What Struggle Brings

A collection of poetry, art, and prose.

Kevin Faulkner

ISBN: 979-8-218-07840-9

"There's beauty in what struggle brings,
but I just can't seem to see."

Acknowledgments

With all of my heart, I must first give proper thanks to Ellen Everett - a wonderful poet, herself. Without her, this might not have ever happened. I had always known that I liked to write, but she is the one who knew that I was a writer. *I wrote a book because she believed in me.* Although her and I's story has come to an end, I am forever grateful for the good that she brought into my life. She is the sweetest person I have ever met, and even still my biggest fan. Thank you so much Ellen. I can't even begin to explain the impact that you have had on me. If my life could be broken up into chapters, I think that you would be my favorite one. I love you, always.

To my mother, you would give the world to me if you could. But even better, you gave me my life. You have supported me in countless ways since the day I was born, and even now you would drop everything in a heartbeat if I ever came to you in a time of need. My greatest wish is that one day I will be able to repay the many favors. You are worth more than gold. I hope you know just how important you are to me.

To my father, our relationship hasn't always been the best. At times, quite strained and distant. But I will be the luckiest man alive if I turn out to be half the man that you are. I thank God everyday, that you are half of who I am. I love you immensely, and could never thank you enough for all of the hard work you have done to provide for me, and the rest of the family. I admire you in more ways than you might know.

As for everyone else, my siblings and friends, *every person that I have met and spent time with*, thank you as well. You have made me who I am. It has been a world of experience - the good, the bad, the lot of it - but I am grateful. I am so very grateful.

: Table of Contents

Section 1: *The Dark*

The Dark Introduction 18
A Reason to Write 22
Learning Curve 24
Instability 26
Untethered 27
Self-Protection 29
Things to Find 30
Lost Out in the Open 32
The Real First Page 37
Who are I? 38
Aggravated 40
Sometimes 44
Same Old Shit 46
God 48
Swinging 51
Shut It 54
Over-Thought 56
Escapism 57
Keeps Going 58
Plastered 61
Better Off 62
Patterns 67
I Don't Care 69
Tired 70
A Modern Man 73
Be Better 77
I Just Want to Fly 81
I Need to Get Right 85

Section 2: *The Haze*

The Haze Introduction	90
Little Pond	94
What Do I Want?	96
Addict	99
Stitched	100
"Remember That"	103
But What Do I Know?	105
More Than Just a Moment	108
Am I Not Strong Enough?	109
What's the Point?	111
Timekeeper	112
Untitled	113
Twisted	115
This Cell That I Call Home	117
In Time	118
In Desperate Need of Truth	120
Spirit	122
Just Keep Moving On	124
Hard to Love	126
Patchwork	129
Conflicted	130
Growing Pains	132
Be Free	136
Psychedelics	141
Truth	142
Sparked	144
Worth Fighting For	145
One Day	146
I've Got This Life to Live	148
The Sun	151
Some Fresh Air	152
It's About Time	153
Call Me Sometime	157
Opportune	158

If I Die Today 159
Wonder 161
Here Comes More Rain 163
Don't Wait Any Longer 165
Cover 167
Living Single 168
How to Love 170

Section 3: *The Light*

The Light Introduction 176
Not Nothing 180
Idyll-d Eyes 181
There is a Reason 182
By Experience 184
You Just Have to Look for Heaven 185
Thank You 186
Don't Get Too Lost to Fly 189
Home 190
Fly Forever 191
Gentle Giants 193
A Reluctant Glow 194
Shhh 195
Positive Affirmations 196
Damned 198
Found It 200
Find It 202
Flower Girl 205
Grateful 207
Let Us Live Like You 209
CAPS LOCK 210
Never 212
Again 214
Let's Go Back to Walter Hill 217

Our Final Night 218
Lovely Lady 219
Hold My Hand 220
Crossing Paths 223
Gentle Terms 224
Step by Step 225
Only if You Allow It 227
Never Hesitate to Speak 228
Re-Connection 231
True Godly Type 233
Art 234
They'll Come and Go 235
Believe 236
Once a Distant Prayer 239
Aged Like Wine 240
Love is Life 242
Keep Hope 244
We'll Be Okay 246
A letter to my readers 247

It is impossible to encapsulate the entirety of someone's life into words; to describe every moment, thought, trauma, and joy. Not everything is meant to be said, but maybe only felt, touched, and tasted. *Experienced.* However, I will try my best. Because life can be a beautiful mess, rife with circumstances that will shatter a soul if one is not grounded. I surely wasn't. I had floated around without any real sense of purpose for a long time. Yet, by the grace of everything good, I have found myself where I am now; full of love and gratitude for the lessons I have learned along the way. *Every moment.*

For a long time I felt *cursed* or *tormented*, as if my heart and mind were destined to live in a constant state of chaos and disorder. *I was not handling it well.* But I have learned and grown, realizing that much of this "Hell" was of my own creation. My anxiety was the end result of an overactive and unfettered mind. I have definitely experienced enough heartbreak throughout my life to know how badly it can hurt. But in truth, I have been equally blessed as well. For longer than I would like to admit, though, I ignored the good almost entirely and let only the negative side of things fester inside of my mind. *I am not alone in this.*

I have a sincere compassion for anyone experiencing their life in a similar manner, and feel compelled to help in any way that I can. Perhaps my raw and honest thoughts here will do just that. Maybe they won't. At the very least, I hope they might validate your feelings and showcase that things will turn around if you allow them to. Furthermore, there are a few subtle shifts in one's perspective that can open up the door to peace, even in the most tormented of souls. *As long as you choose to heal.*

Life is anything but a burden. It is a gift, simply waiting to be received. However, in order to do that, you have to let go of the bullshit and nonsense that is weighing you down. This book, these words and images, is me releasing mine. *Finally.* Or at least what has boiled to the surface thus far. It is a lifelong journey.

I am no moral authority by any means. Surely this will be evident to you as you comb your way through this book. What I am is a person, as imperfect as the next, who was hurt and seemingly *broken* for a long time; aimlessly swerving through the inevitable, with a chip the size of Jupiter on my shoulder. Take some of my heavier thoughts and self judgments with a grain of salt, though, because I have always been my own harshest critic. But who isn't, really? It's unfortunate how easily the mind can wander into patterns of negative self-talk.

In all honesty, however, I have been a good man. Or at least I have tried to be. Just, at times, I may have been a bit rebellious and misguided on my search for truth and purpose. All the while, judging myself harshly by the deeply rooted standards of my rigid, religious upbringing, d*espite having lost faith in nearly everything.* I was a hot mess to say the least. But you live and learn, suffering the karma of poor decisions as you go. Until one day, you either die or choose to see the light. *I pray that you see the light.*

I have tried my best to organize these poems in some sort of meaningful way. However, my process of healing has been anything but a clean progression. My life, my world, and my perspectives have been all over the place; whipped and whirled in every direction, *as is the way of life.* Looking back, though, I wouldn't change a thing. Because I wouldn't be the person that I am today without every twist and turn that this journey has offered me. Nevertheless, it sure can make it tough to tell the story. Be gentle with me, be gentle with yourself, and buckle up for the ride. Much Love.

This book has been divided into three sections; The Dark, The Haze, and The Light. Each of these sections resemble different stages of life, or potential patterns of thought, *that we all can get caught in.* Some of this content is heavy, and some of it not so nice...

Undoubtedly there is venom in these pages. However, there is also love, acceptance, and delight. If you are a person who is easily triggered, or in a place where absorbing any more negativity into your life would be too much for you, please skip ahead. Come back to The Dark, or even The Haze, whenever you are ready.

These feelings are honest, and I believe sharing them is important; *beyond even my own ability to understand why.* But take them at your own pace. My intention has only ever been for healing, however half of that process is understanding the darkness that resides within you. So do as you do, and go as you go. I just wanted to let you know that as you flip through these pages, it gets a little easier :)

A final note, many of these poems, *if not most,* were written to be read aloud. So for the best effect, keep that in mind as you read, *or perform,* them to yourself. *God Bless.*

What Struggle Brings

WHAT IS THIS shroud that is consuming me? THAT IN THE DAY is stealing my LIGHT, AND in the NIGHT is stealing SLEEP? That is tightening MY CHEST so much, TO BREATHE I have to scream. THAT HAS captivated thoughts in patterns, incomplete. so that TOMORROW I might think again RIGID and GIVE AWAY my freedom TO this darkness. Where DID I go WRONG?

The Dark

What is this shroud that is consuming me?
That in the day is stealing light,
and in the night is stealing sleep?
That is tightening my chest,
so much, to breathe I have to scream.
That has captivated thoughts
in patterns, rigid, incomplete.
So that tomorrow I might think again
and give away my freedom
to this darkness.
Where did I go wrong? ...

The Dark Introduction

It feels odd to try and offer any type of advice from my position. I'm not an expert with a PhD in psychology, or a trained therapist or life coach. I'm just a normal guy, who has likely only suffered the pains of a somewhat normal life. However, I can't help but speak my truth. I haven't always been that way though. In many regards, one of my biggest problems was my inability, or unwillingness, to voice my vulnerabilities and ask for help when I needed it. That has led me to some pretty dark places that I hope no one else ever has to visit. So here I am, putting my heart on the line, hoping that you might be able to learn from my mistakes instead. *There have been plenty.*

I almost wish that I could tell you that my life has been the hardest by comparison, or that the world has only ever given me shit. That would make it much easier to justify the sadness I have felt. Not to say, of course, that I haven't experienced any hardship or been wronged by others in many ways. I have. But in all honesty, I have lived a fairly pleasant life, with countless blessings and experiences provided to me. It has been quite difficult for me to reconcile those two realities, though, without either denying my feelings or seeming ungrateful for the good. It is nearly impossible to strike that balance fairly, and like a pendulum, I have swung in every direction while pursuing it.

Nearly impossible *is not* impossible, however, and I am far closer now than I have ever been; mostly due to a few subtle shifts in my perspectives and outlook that were taught to me by others. I hope to extend these gifts to you as well, if you are open and willing to hear them. Because truthfully, no one ever has to suffer *indefinitely*.

Be that as it may, suffering and sadness are fairly normal responses to have when things go awry, and in those moments they should never be suppressed. Otherwise, like me, you'll only end up prolonging the misery. But they are also emotions that you should try your best to not get stuck in. The question is, if you are feeling trapped, how do you get out? I never went to therapy. I probably should have, but I am far too stubborn for that. But the beauty of therapy, from what I have heard, is that it helps address the roots of your problems first. This, in turn, allows you to heal whatever has branched off from them. It's important not to skip that step, or else anything that you manage to pluck from the vine will inevitably grow back.

In many ways, poetry has been my therapy. I didn't intend it to be. I just sort of fell into it. But once I started to write, I couldn't stop. It was so freeing. *However, I didn't plan on publishing a book.* I only wrote most of these poems to help organize my unrelenting, intrusive thoughts of anxiety and self-doubt. The idea of the book only really materialized when I recognized how influential these poems had been to me. Furthermore, *despite much of their negativity,* that some good could potentially be extracted from them as a whole.

I have been slightly fearful of releasing them though. Not because of what they might make you think of me. But instead, how a few things in here might be construed as airing out drama, or painting some people in a negative light.

I'm not looking to place blame on anyone for anything. My biggest problem ultimately has been myself, and how I have reacted to things. Having said that, many issues of mine stemmed from childhood; *as they often do, unfortunately.* Everybody's family fucks them up in one way or another. But even so, I love my family dearly. They are all truly wonderful people who have given me so much, and they deserve every ounce of grace, love, and respect that this world has to offer. I hold them in the highest regard. I just had to get some shit off my chest, is all. That aside, I'll share with you some of my story, hoping that it may inspire the courage in you to dig up your own roots and set your heart free.

I was raised in a very religious home, with God at the center of everything we did. Or at least that was our intention. *We tried our best.* But with that lifestyle came a pressure for perfection that was simply unattainable, and with every slip in the wrong direction came a sense of shame, stemming mostly from within ourselves. This kind of internal tension can make even the strongest spirit snap and hope to die in a whimper. It isn't pleasant.

In our case, however, it led to fighting in the home. There was absolutely love in my family, but there was an equal amount of turmoil for a time. Nobody was innocent. But our foundation was being broken, shattered and eventually divided. Imagine our sense of shame then, *when my parents split.* Coupled, of course, with the whispered disgrace from within our community. Everyone was always very kind and generous to us, but we knew that we were the tainted bunch, *divorced from the grace of God.* Or that's how it seemed.

We also moved a lot when I was young. That alone would have been enough to cause some issues. Perpetually being the new kid was never easy. I had lost a lot of friends, *through no fault of my own*, and grew afraid of getting close to anyone because of it. Although I had become somewhat used to living as an "outcast," this felt so much worse. Because when we finally moved again, *this time away from my father*, I was bereft. Because, not only did I lose him, I lost all connection to God; *and with that my purpose in life.* The depression running rampantly through my home was proof enough to me that we had been forgotten. Plucked from *His* presence and left to wilt. I raged against this, *quietly.* I was so angry. How could this have happened to us? God was dead. *He* had to be. Or at least *He* was to me.

I still managed to hide behind a smile though. I didn't want to extend my sour feelings onto my already heartbroken family. So I pushed them down, secretly suffocating under the weight of it all; desperately searching for an escape. *Which I found,* when for the first time in my life I had managed to gain some popularity in my new town. *Despite never thinking that I deserved it*, I took it for what it was and used it to chase after every pleasure imaginable. I intentionally broke every rule and standard that I had been held to before, hoping that this was somehow the road to happiness. But it only led me further and further astray, and into the arms of my own toxic relationships, which set in stone my trust issues and cemented the idea in my heart that love didn't truly exist. Or perhaps, that I just wasn't worthy of it. This section, *The Dark*, is some of what I felt.

A Reason to Write

Well...

I guess I'll give this a try.
An attempt to explain myself,
to myself.
As I write things down,
dissecting and learning
from the things
that I might say.

Words that have never been muttered
from my lips before.
Things that I could never
bring myself to say.

Thoughts
that I have gotten
so lost in,
that the weaves and turns are
tangled,
webbed,
and wrought in disarray.

Maybe this will help.

Maybe soon
I'll sleep well at night.

Maybe soon...
I'll be sure of one thing,
me.
Who I am,
what I want,
and who I strive to be.

Because
that's really something I should figure out.
That's really something I should know now.
As I try to build a life and home,
trying to make something of myself.

Maybe,
I'll be finally well.

Learning Curve

What makes you a real father?
It's more than sharing blood.
You have to be there for your children
and show your children love.
You'll be their rock that never falters,
helping bear the storms to come.
Yet each new day is still unknown,
that bond you've built is strong.
You'll lift them up onto your shoulders,
like you did when they were young.
Then one day with a heavy heart,
you'll watch them do it on their own.
They'll teach the things you taught to them,
your time together showing.
Because most important, over all,
you were there when they were growing.
But what's it like to have a father?
I'm not the one to say.
Because when our struggles hit the fan,
my father didn't stay.

They'll teach the things you taught to them,
your time together showing.
Because most important, over all,
you were there when they were growing.

Instability

Change..
Change..
Change..
We're moving places.
Here's another chance
to make new friends
and see new faces.
Go introduce yourself.

But I often stayed inside my shell.
Because with every move
we moved again,
and losing friends was hell.
So I just stopped caring.

Or at least I tried to...

Untethered

What's another fight?
What's another morning woke to screaming?
What's more "war torn" shame and pride,
to a pair of young eyes.

I didn't know what words to say.
"This time," was just like any.
But "this time," we parted ways,
and then things changed forever.

We packed our bags, moved out of state,
and then everything felt different.
Everything except our names.
Even our souls were quivering.

Sure,
we still *had* a home,
but had no place...
And although we went to church
no words could stop our fall from "grace."

And my whole world untethered.

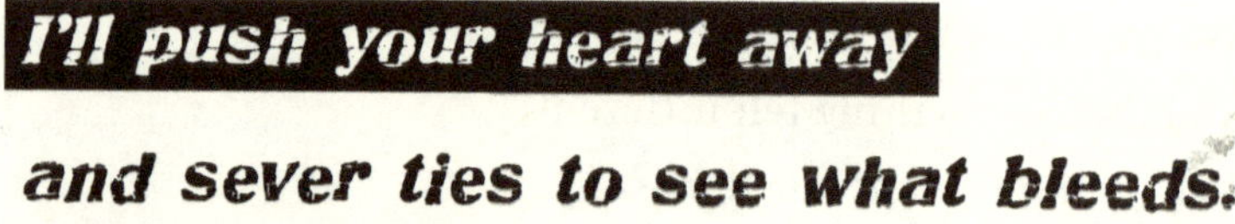

I'll push your heart away
and sever ties to see what bleeds.
Me, usually.

Self-Protection

With...

A heart that's lacking love,
a mind that's lacking trust,
a soul that's lacking "anything worth fighting for,"
I cannot give a fuck.

I put my shields up.

No.
Please don't get close to me.
I'll push your heart away
and sever ties to see what bleeds.

Me, usually.

Things to Find

There are things I've got to know,
but they've never been told to me.
I've got to learn them on my own,
because I'm grown now.

I'm grown now.
Shit, I'm grown now.
And I've been *standing on my own two feet*,
barely seeing clear.
Caught up in the haze I'm blowing,
because I'm barely breathing air.

Man, my head is feeling fuzzy.
Ma'am I'm sorry if I stare,
because I really wasn't there for a minute.
I was lost inside my head.
I left my body feeling dead.

I was well for a moment,
but now it's back to work instead.
Oh, how I dread it.
I just want to rest my head.
But it keeps on going,
never finding peace.

At least I've got a *flow* that comforts me.
An outlet for my thoughts.

It's who I want to be.
Sincerely, *it's the real me.*
But you'll never know him.

I just hope you'll notice me,
because I've been noticing,
depression setting in.
I think I need a sedative.
Please stick it in my skin,
so I can stop the spinning.
Stop myself from sinning.
It doesn't matter the cost,
because, I feel lost

and I really need to find myself.

Lost Out in the Open

You know it's funny...
How my house is not my home.
It may be where I live,
but it's far from where I've grown.

And every day...
Where I'm from is more unknown.
It's left me guessing where I'm going.
It's got me stressing every moment.
It's made me realize
that I'm broken.

I think it's the reason
that I can't stop smoking.
I can't stop drinking.
I can't stop floating with no direction,
like I'm lost out in the open,
with no sign that the earth is slowing.

While
I'm sitting still,
relaxed and open
to free thought,
because, *damn*, this bud is potent.

I need to quit.

But who am I kiddin'?
What am I jokin'?
This drug induced *sense of self*
is far from being over.

Years of me have led to this.
I should pray for a couple more.
But if God is real...
He'd leave me here,
because He'd know that I can soar.
Higher than my doubt permits,
and what I've seen before.

There's good in me.
I swear there is.
It's bleeding from my core.
I just need a way to focus it,
and that's what my art's been for.
I've been told that it's my gift,
but really, it's something more.

It's a love.
It's a light.
It's an outlet from inside.
It's something that lets me breathe.
That something has kept me alive.

And it gives me hope.

For a better me just click *reload*.
But the world it loves to change.
Things evolve and switch their roles.

Time has passed...
I've gotten older,
but I'm hanging by the ropes.
I'm trying to support myself,
but it's hard,
I'm a young adult.

Who's still in school.
Still playing by the rules.
Still trying to be myself.
But who am I?
I'm just a fool.

Who is probably going nowhere,
because I'm stuck and still impaired.
Because...
Life, it isn't easy,
and nobody said it's fair.
But it's kind of getting to me.
My heart's stripped and it's bare.
But really, there's no point to this.

Because *nobody really cares*.

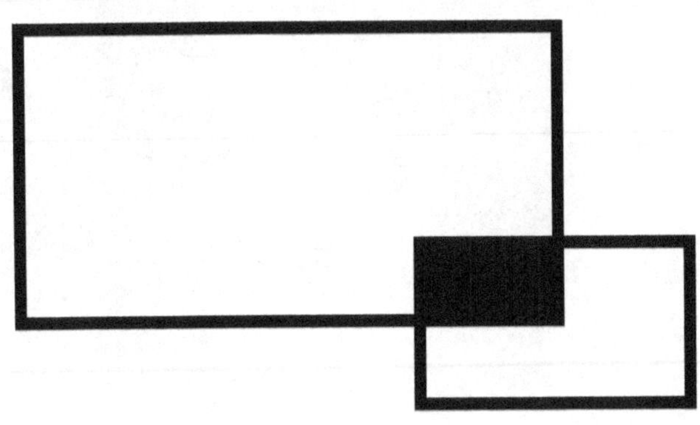

I NEED TO QUIT.
But who am I kiddin'?
What am I jokin'?
This drug induced sense of self
is far from being over.

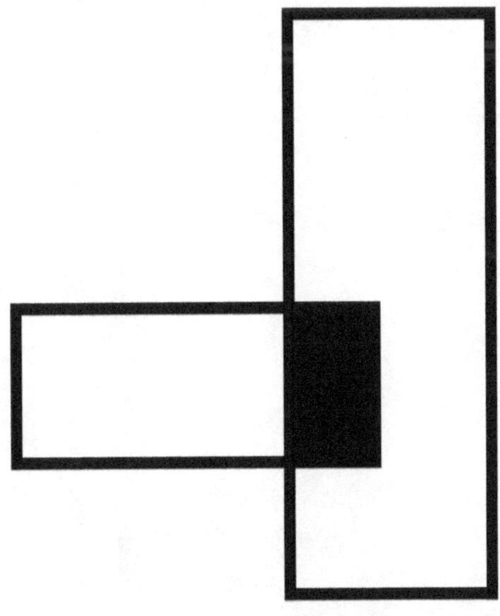

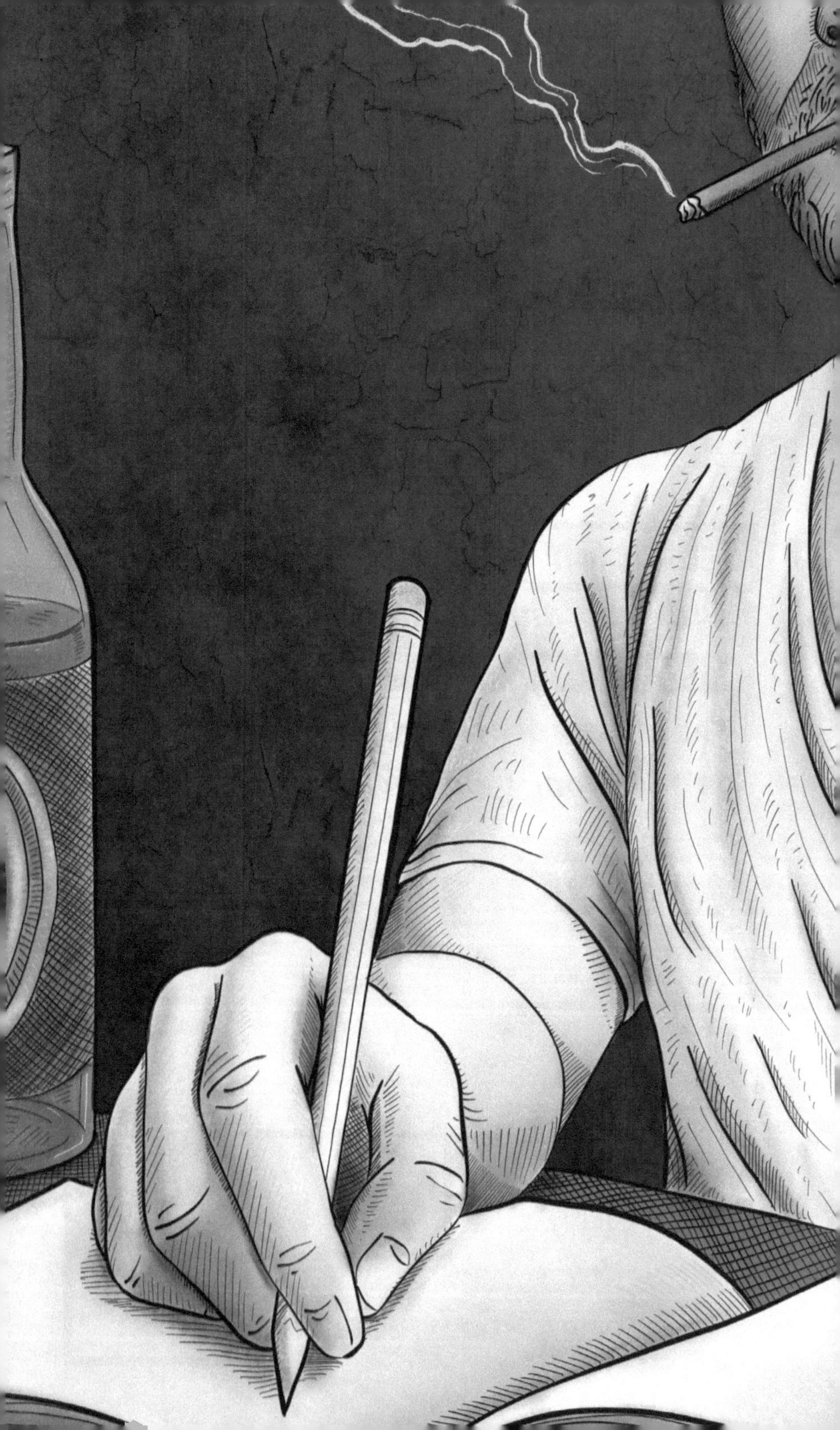

THE REAL FIRST PAGE

I got a journal today,
and I think I need to write in it.
There's potential in these empty lines.
It's something I can work with.

So,
I've been writing,
but still I'm lost in thought.
And *they've* been
rocky,
rotten.
Really nothing new for me,
it's often.

But it's not enough.

Because I keep numbing all my cells,
so I can tolerate myself,
and slow the thoughts down so they're tangible.

I've got a handle on it.

But I've barely got my grip.
I could try to readjust,
but I might fuck around and slip.

So I'll take "not enough."

Who are I?

My smile is getting tired.
It's a shame that it's been fake.
I barely make it through most days,
but rarely show it on my face.

Because,
I don't like exposing weakness,
so I'd rather play this game.
Hide my pain.
Then, fucking, duck out,
so my image stays maintained.

As this cool, calm, and collected man
with the knowledge of *his place*,
throughout this *cosmic webbed entanglement.*
This pale blue dot in space.
That's more complex than we can comprehend
with supplemented faiths.
In our Gods, Kings, and Governance
that claim to know their way,
while often paving roads to hell,
until they're violently replaced.
By just another saving grace,
who will probably be worse...

But I'm just another guy,
so who am I to claim their worth?

Who am I to cast a judgment
of, *fucking*, anything on Earth?
Because I'm truly far perfect,
and acknowledging that hurts.

But, at least I'm feeling something, *right?*

My body's barely working,
but at least I sleep through most my nights.
While ignoring my anxiety
of squandering potential,
in our truth-gilded society,
that's riddled with deceit and greed,
then masked because we call it free.

I guess it's just like me,
saving face and dead inside.
But we'll never learn or grow
until we see our *dimming light.*

Aggravated

Look...

I don't know
where I've been going,
but I'm going still.
But I've been suffering,
I'm buffering,
struggling.
Thought, *"I might kill myself."*

But...
I haven't.
I'm breathing.
My heart's still beating.
If I cut my skin, I'm bleeding.
But, fuck me.
These thoughts repeat.

So,
I've been barely hanging on,
but I've been *strong,*
and I've been *woke.*
So I've been *well,*
but I've been *broke.*
So I'm escaping in this smoke
that I'm inhaling,
coughing,

choking on.
I'm higher than I'm showing,
but I'm lower than I'm leading on.
I'm moments from imploding.

But,
that's really nothing new.
I'm in hell and I've been through it.
I've discovered who I am.
I fucking hate him.
I'm a screw-up.
I'm another piece of shit
who's going nowhere.
I'm a loser.

There's this doubt inside of me
that I can't shake,
and it's *consuming* every part of me,
that used to mean something.
It's left me empty.

I'm trying to find my place,
but it's vacant.
I've felt abandoned lately.

I've been separating myself from the crowds,
because they agitate me.
I've been fading back into the shadows.
I've been contemplating

life and all its battles.
They're tragic,
but somehow captivating.

I just can't escape this mental state,
and, shit, I'm tired of waiting.
Good won't come around.
You've got to make it.
But, I'm lacking patience,
lacking training.

I need to relax.
But,
FUCK
I'm aggravated.

I need to relax.
But, FUCK
I'm aggravated.

Sometimes

Sometimes,
I struggle to be happy.
Which sometimes,
I think is overreacting.
But it feels like *more than real* to me.
Which is funny,
because I feel like I can't feel a thing.

And *there's beauty in what struggle brings,*
but I just can't seem to see.

Because with this weight that's on my chest,
it's getting harder just to breathe.
It's getting harder to stay motivated,
harder just to dream.
I'm just getting sick and tired
of this person known as *me.*
Who's been running fucking wild,
because I can,
because I'm *free.*

Forgetting about consequence
and the legacies I leave,
because it's just *too much to think about.*
Too much to interweave
with my quandaries of the universe
that challenged my beliefs.

That left me feeling helpless,
feeling tangled in my grief.

Sort of like
I'm being strangled
by my doubt of truth or peace,
because there's bloody battles every day,
and all we win is greed.
Which only carries further on
then swallows what we see.
Then corruption riddles governments
and quickly roots its seeds.
Spreading power webs that rule the world
with leaders fat and greased,
who let the patterns fumble on–
and then history repeats.

It's sad.

But it never skips a beat.
So my hope is quickly fading
that goodwill can still compete.
That our hearts will change the world,
or will simply wither from deceit.
I fear our story's nearly over
with an end left incomplete.

So yeah,
sometimes I struggle to be happy–
but maybe I'm just overreacting.

Same Old Shit

I laugh away depression
like it's normal.

Because I've found that it's *easier*
to try and just ignore it.

But here I am,
bothered by the same old shit.

It's just another day in Paradise.
I'm here for it.

It's just another
day in Paradise.
I'm here for it.

God

I'm so mad at you.
Assuming you're even real.
But you won't take the time to prove it,
so how *else* am I to feel?

How come you won't talk to me?

I guess I'm just not worthy.
I've been trying to keep in touch...
But I'm losing hope. I'm giving up...
Because I have cried enough prayers to you.
If you're there, you've seen me.
If you're there, you've heard me call.
But you don't give a fuck at all, huh?
Didn't you make all of this?
The good, the bad, the lot of it?
There is blood that's on YOUR hands,
and in a second you could stop this shit.

Assuming you're even there...

But maybe I've been wasting my time,
talking to walls,
talking to nothing.
Fuck it.
Goodbye "God."

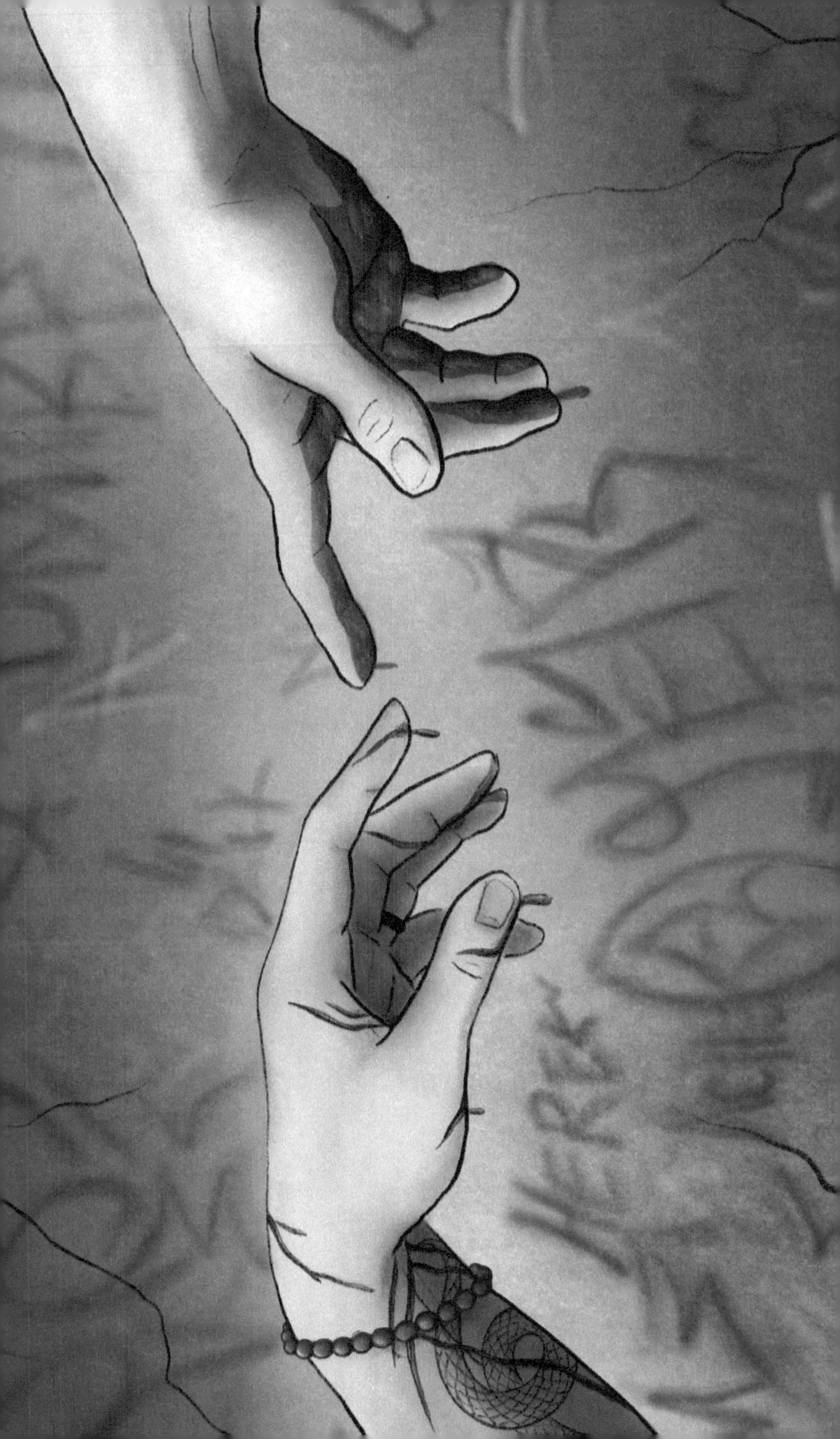

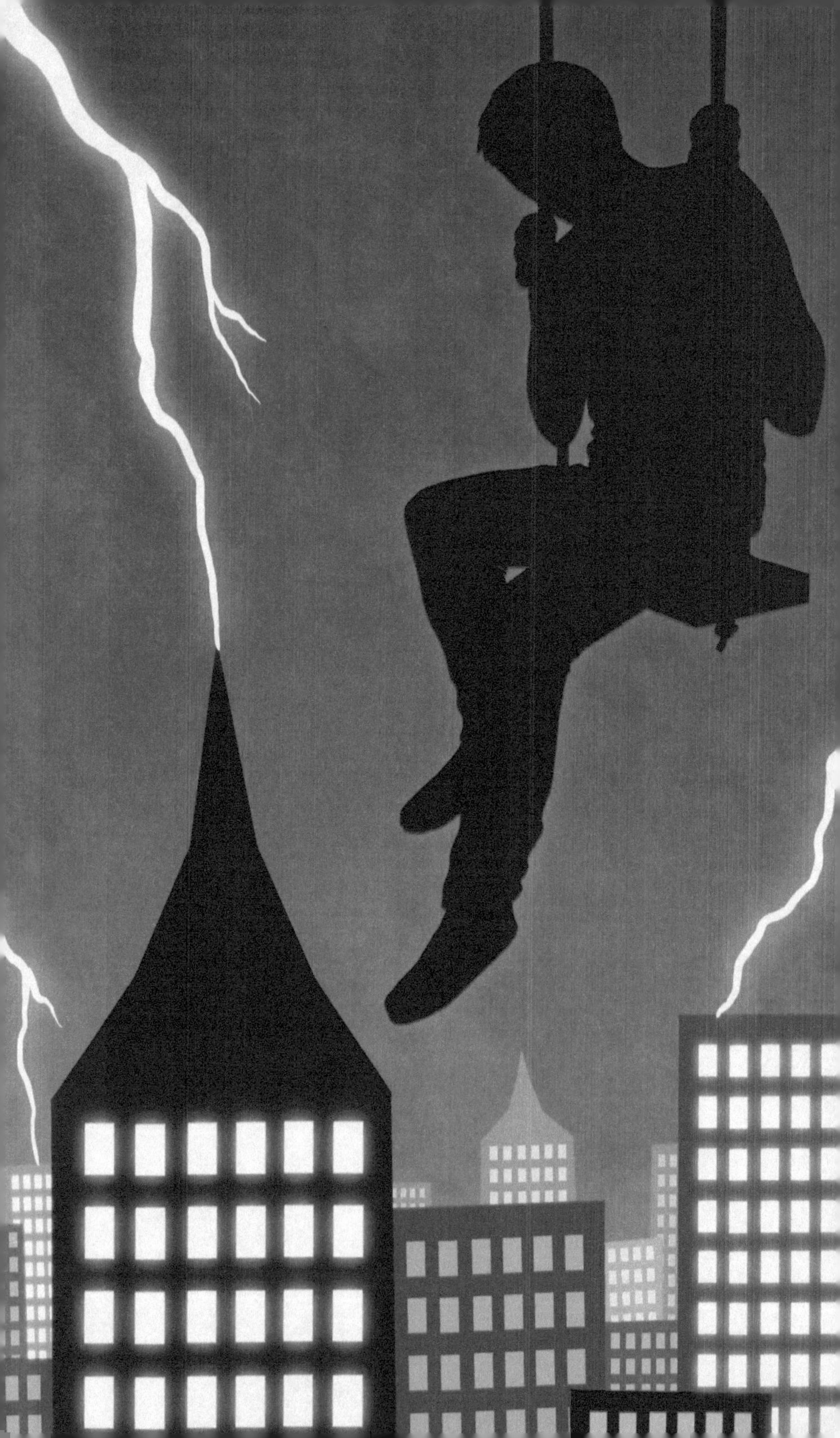

SWINGING

There are days I want to die.
And there are days I want to cry out
with pure laughter, because I'm overjoyed.
But the balance,
I just can't get right.
I'm swinging *back and forth*.
I'm fucking tired,
but can't sleep at night.

Because I don't want to dream.

Because it reminds me of the pretty things
and how they're ripped away in just a second.
And how that second breaks a lifetime.
Then cuts the lifeline to your mental health
and slowly lets you suffocate,
under the weight of your own suffering,
but for me it's just the waiting.
I can't take it.

So,
just take me now
and end it all.
I'm barely breathing as it is.
So go ahead, *let me fall*.
Let me shatter what you know of me.
Let my habits drain the energy

that makes the blood pump through my veins.
That keeps me barely hanging on
and makes me lie,
saying *I'm sane.*
Saying *I'm strong enough to suffer this.*
This trick from my own brain,
that makes me see the world for what it is,
or what it's not,
they seem the same.

Because, the scene is captured raw
then filters down to pride and shame.
The jagged essence of my selfishness
that clots, and keeps my blood un-fallen rain.
Bringing life to *nothing,*
while preserving the mental strain
that is taxing all my systems,
further splintering my frame.
While it slithers through my consciousness
and *eats away* at everything I know and love.

My future's dim.
My present's dark.
I feel its presence,
flames have sparked
inside my chest.
It wants my heart.
Because it wasn't charred enough...

So, fucking, *burn it 'til it's ash,*
so I can't feel this way again.
Because if things stay as they've been,
then I *won't see* tomorrow's end.

But...
I'm sure tomorrow I'll be fine.
Because I'll swing back,
or just pretend.

Shut It.

Shut it down.
Shut it down.

You've thought enough about this.

You've spent enough time grieving
over things you can't control.
So, shut it down
or you'll fall deeper down this hole,
and you'll be lost forever.

Shut it down.
Please.

Please.

Over-thought

All the way to the bitter end,
I'll likely think myself to death.
I'll likely turn too many corners
broadly mapping unhinged stress.

I'll likely get lost in my patterns,
as to me, they're just old friends,
who have been with me for years
and now are comfortable here.
I can't upend them.

They might not want what's best for me,
but, God, I can depend on them.
Even when it's them who run me down.

-There's much to think about-

Escapism

Maybe I should just ignore this...
Pain is just for a moment, right?
So there's no need to go exploring it.
Emotions have a riddled bite
that fester in abhorrence,
and I'm bored of it.

But...
I'd really, rather just not feel them.
So maybe I'll conceal
this bitter state
and take a break
from what seems real,
and numb myself into oblivion,
forever sheltered from my fear.
I could spend a lifetime dormant,
without ever, really feeling anything...

Sounds just like a dream, huh?
But what sounds worse than our realities?
That come with tribulations
that are trialled by our tragedies.
That often find an end
in ways that break a heart,
or make it bleed...
So why go work for anything?
When nothing, ever, sets you free.

Keeps Going

Around and around I go.
Sometimes fast
and sometimes slow.
Just trying to live
and trying to grow.
Hiding all of my pain,
fearing that it will show.
And hoping that it will pass,
because really you never know
what tomorrow might bring,
which events will unfold.
What someone might say,
bitter or even cold,
or how you will respond.
I was born with a heart of gold.
But life chips that away,
until you're left with just the mold.
Until you're barely hanging on,
barely breathing,
feeling frozen.
And left with no escape,
punching bricks and just unloading.
While you're screaming at the world,
and at yourself because you're broken.
Damn,
I'm tired of this road that I'm on,
but it just keeps going.

WORLD,

I DON'T KNOW WHAT IT IS THAT KEEPS ME FROM GOING CRAZY. SNAPPING AND BREAKING MY HANDS AGAINST A BRICK WALL OUT OF ANGER. THERE IS SO MUCH ABOUT MY LIFE THAT NO ONE KNOWS ABOUT. WHAT BROUGHT ME TO TENNESSEE, WHAT TURNED ME INTO A "WOMANIZER", WHAT CREATED THE HOT MESS THAT YOU SEE TODAY, BUT KNOW NOTHING ABOUT. PEOPLE ASSUME THAT BECAUSE I AM A NICE PERSON WITH A SMILE ON MY FACE MOST OF THE TIME, THAT I HAVE NEVER KNOWN PAIN. BELIEVE ME, I KNOW PAIN. IT'S WHY I HAVE NUMBED MYSELF FOR YEARS WITH ALCOHOL, WEED, AND LOOSE WOMEN. I HAVE JUST BEEN BOTTLING EVERYTHING UP, UNTIL IT EVENTUALLY COMES OUT AND TEARS ME DOWN. AGAIN, THAT'S NOW. THE BOURBON THAT I'M DRINKING SURELY DOESN'T HELP. IT'S AN ESCAPE, BUT I STAY TRAPPED IN MY HEAD. TORMENTED BY THE PAST, AND TERRIFIED OF THE FUTURE. FUCK THE WORLD, I'M SICK OF IT. BUT I'M STILL HERE AND I'M NOT GOING ANYWHERE. I DON'T KNOW WHAT IT IS THAT KEEPS ME SANE, BUT I THANK IT. HOWEVER, I CURSE AND LOATHE IT ALL THE SAME. FUCK IT, FUCK ME, FUCK YOU.

LOVE,
KEVIN

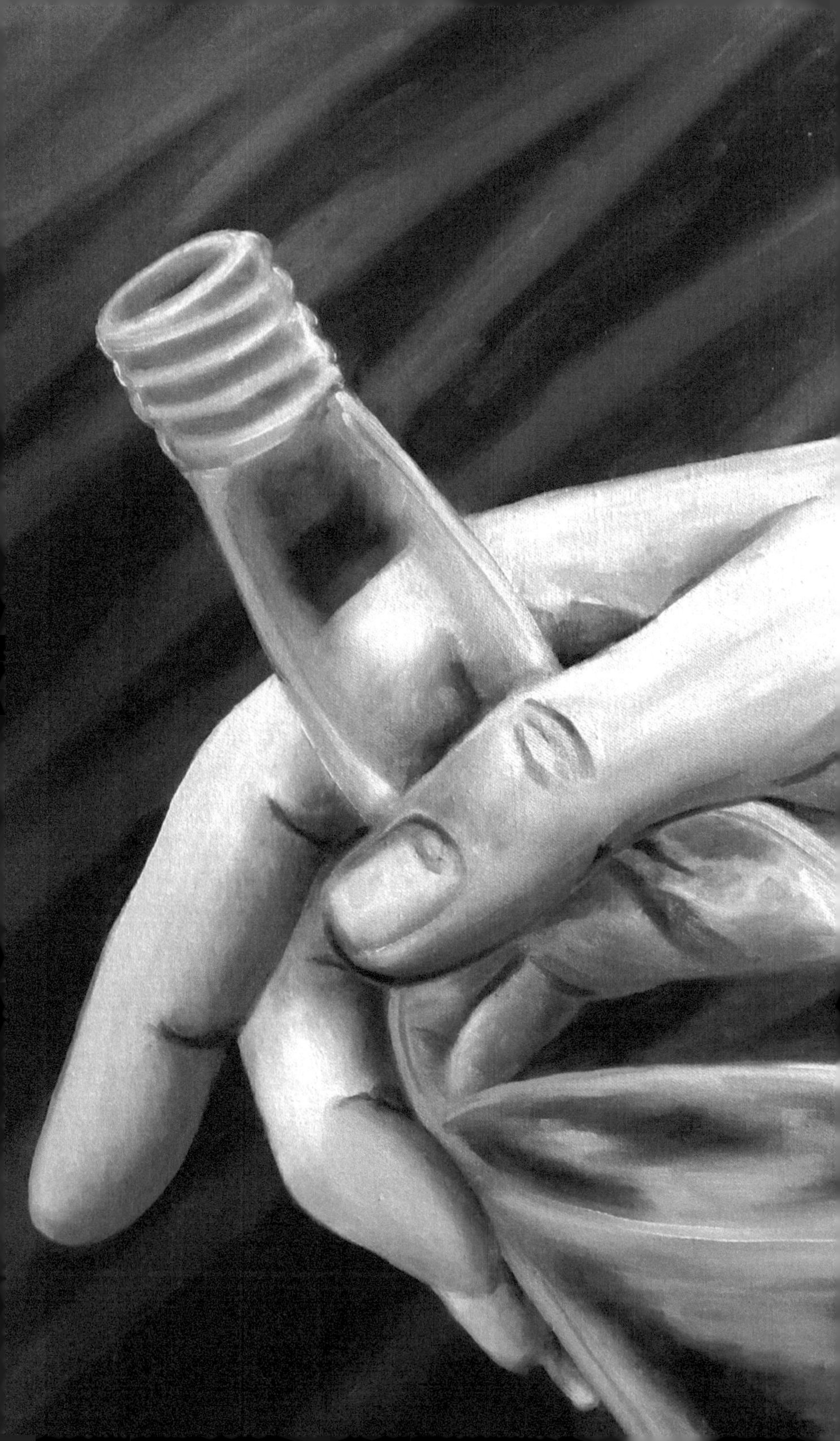

Plastered

I like my alcohol to hit strong,
so I'll hit back.
Make me feel the burn,
so I can torch the night,
forget tact.
Make me lose control,
because I don't want it right now.
Because lately it's been trolling,
tolling,
tugging me down.
And I just,
I need a break
for a moment, or hour.
I just... need an escape
from myself, I'm a coward.
I'm just,
tired of acting fake
like I've been strong and empowered.
Like I've been laser-*fucking*-focused,
not just running around.
Like a chicken with its head cut off,
no vision or sound.
Because these thoughts here have me blocked up,
but I smile for crowds.
And I'm just, *tired.*
I just need a drink.
I just need to clear my head,
so that there's room for me to think.

Better Off

"Roll the dope and pass it."
But, God, I feel fucked up...
God, I've got to cash my luck in.
I've got a God that's looking up,
because this is higher than I thought I'd be.
The edge is looking interesting,
because I could fucking trip,
and there's the end of me...
But tell me,
who's my enemy
if I'm the one in charge?

If I'm the one that always seemed
to take things way too far.

If I'm the one...
That thinks he's losing touch
'cause his reality's slipping.
His mind has been gifted
by freedom's light.
I'm blind,
but I'm with it.

It could be my guide out of the *trenches.*
But it's been weird...
I feel like
I've already been here.

Like I've been running
through these circles for years...

Because I've been to several dark places
on many jaded occasions,
but I've been
trapped in my mind,
so all that time has been *wasted*.
And now I'm stressing my mortality.
Divine intervention could help me see
that I have the eyes of a dreamer.
A heart for believing
that *we've been good*.
But still my mind's been a cynic.
It's always a critic,
and now what?
It's got something to say?

"Yeah,
quit your bullshit.
I'm the reason you're still standing today.
I've kept you right in place,
won't budge at all.
I've put up walls.
You're safe here.
So quit complaining 'bout your drama.
Man the fuck up.
You're a fuck-up.
Life's been fucked up.

But you're here right?
So deal with it."

Well, I've been trying,
but I'd rather escape it.
I'd rather jump this fucking ship
than sober up from my fading.
I'd rather waste my fucking life away
than deal with my anger,
because I'm in pain,
with open wounds.
I'm in anguish.

But when I'm high
I feel like I've found *salvation,*
'cause I don't feel a thing.
I'm free now.
But this moment's been fleeting
since the beginning.
I can't chase it down.
And I can't, fucking, just enjoy it either.
So,
I guess I'm hopeless.
I guess I'm broken.
I guess I'm better off still smoking.

Fuck me.

"So quit complaining
'bout your drama.
Man the fuck up.
You're a fuck-up.
Life's been fucked up.
But you're here right?
So deal with it."

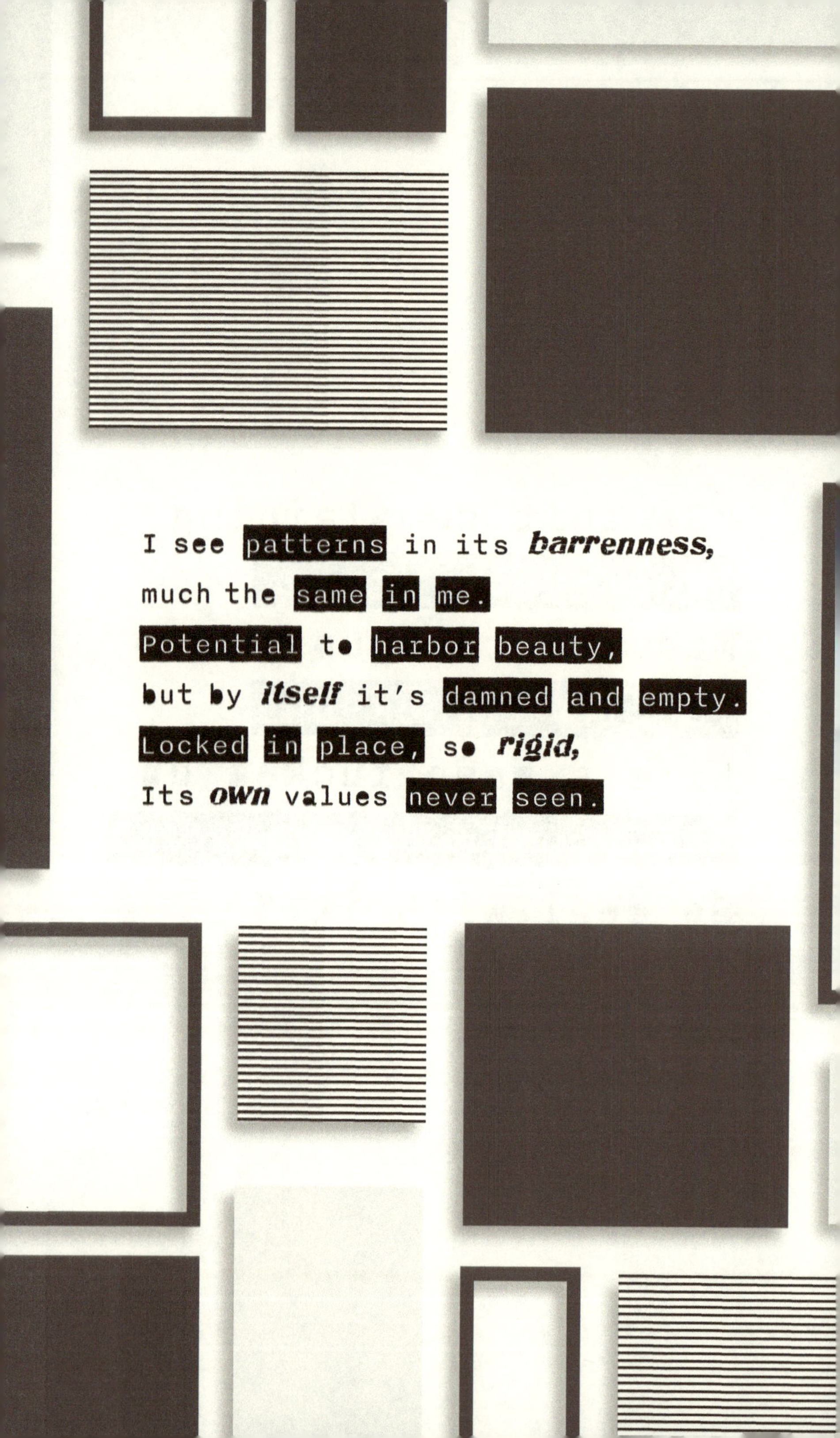

I see patterns in its barrenness,
much the same in me.
Potential to harbor beauty,
but by itself it's damned and empty.
Locked in place, so rigid,
Its own values never seen.

Patterns

Every now and then,
I lean back
and try to look for stars.
But lately I've been locked in
only finding walls with sharp corners.
I've hung those walls with art
to try to give a pop of color,
but it's the empty space
that draws me in.

It's like it feels forgotten.
It's pleading it has more to give.
But things go where they fit
despite their options,
and that's *just the way it is.*

But that doesn't help the empty space.
It doesn't hide its face.
I could make more art today
to fill the place,
but it would likely lose my gaze.

I see patterns in its barrenness,
much the same in me.
Potential to harbor beauty,
but by itself it's damned and empty.

Locked in place, so rigid,
its own values never seen.
But when I close my eyes,
all bets are free.
Those walls are roaring seas.
Expanding into open time,
further than one can see.
Paving through with heart in haste,
as if nothing has ever been holding me back...

But, as I open my eyes,
I see the same patterns.
Dreams shattered,
because some things never change.

I Don't Care.

I don't live within the margins.

I prefer to be out of whack.

Sometimes I may seem far-fetched,

maybe I'm lacking tact.

But I'm *happy* without my margins,

they'll never tell me how to act.

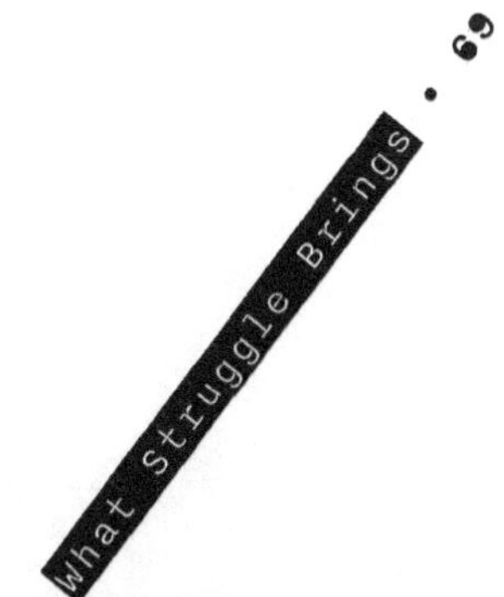

I'm honestly getting tired of trying to understand the world. There are too many variables, too many opposing truths, too many opportunities for good and evil; so many that they can't find balance. What we get is tension, conflict, war, and unending opposition. As if we are "blessed" with stress. It's everywhere.

I'd like to just shut it off, but I can't. I have zero control over the world and its appetite. It will act on its own, and my life is purely a reaction.

As a product of the world, I am subject to its whims, and it will be whimsical. It will be brash. There will be good, and I pray it's plentiful. But there's a good chance that things will descend into chaos.

I am subject to its whims,
and it will be whimsical.
It will be brash.
There will be good,
and I pray it's plentiful.
But there's a good chance
that things will
descend into chaos.

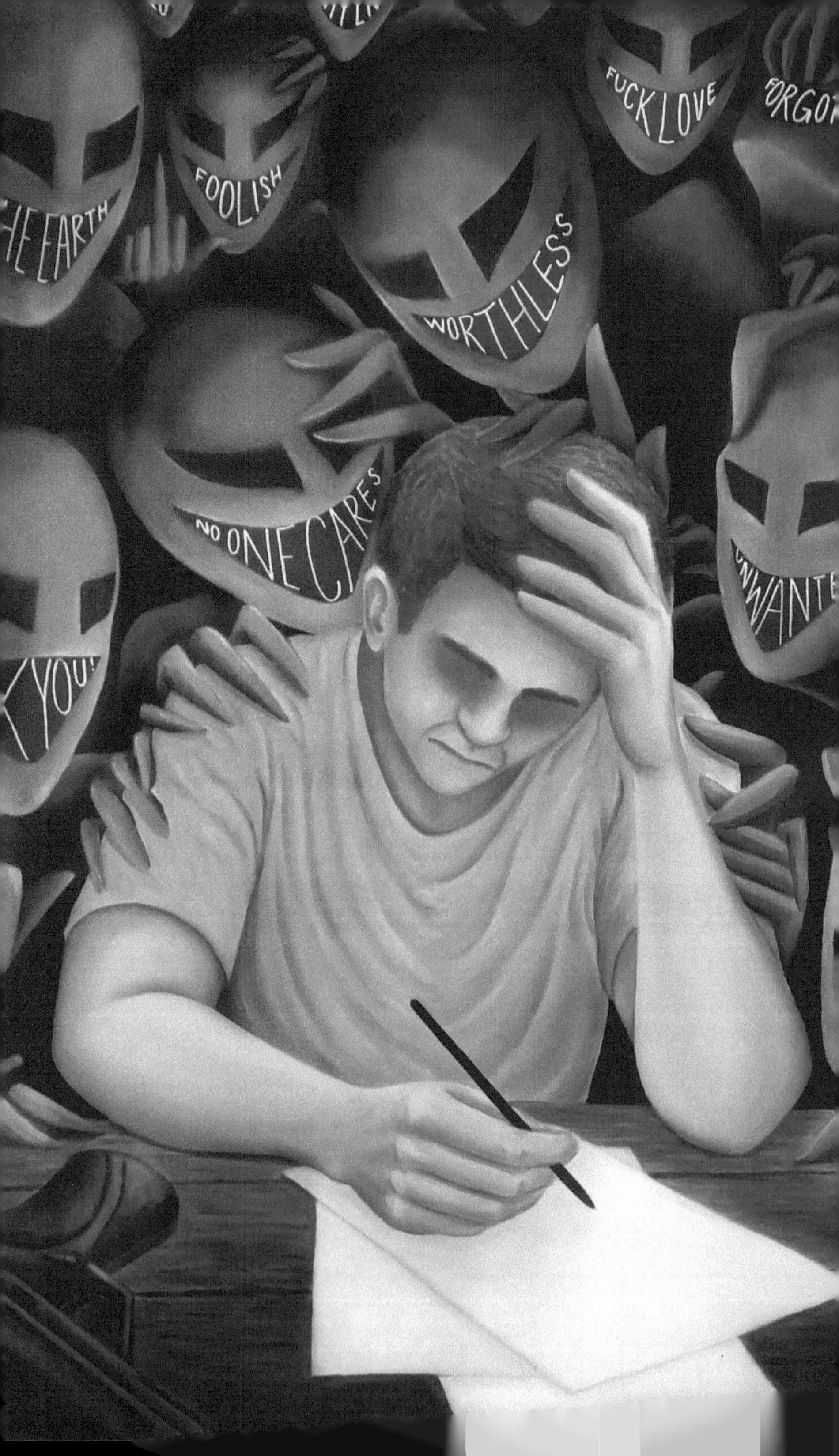

HE EARTH
FOOLISH
FUCK LOVE
ORGOT
WORTHLESS
NO ONE CARES
K YOU
NWANTE

A MODERN MAN

I've got so many faces, like my lying can't stop.
I've done so many drugs,
I'm surprised that I ain't locked up.
I've had so many different streams of thought,
I think they've severed my reality.
I'm caught between the search for peace
and trying to keep my cock up.

I don't know who I am,
because even I don't understand me.
But it hurts to be a man,
because it comes with understanding
that...
No one gives a fuck about,
what you give a fuck about,
and then they wonder why we fuck around,
so fuck them all.

But there's no value in a life that's uninvolved.
Still, I run from love
like I prefer the bitter cold.
'Cause I can tell myself, "I'm comfortable,"
and that problem's solved, right?
"Everything is alright,"
but I can't fucking sleep at night.
These voices in my head keep barking,

"This is what you wanted."
"They're the choices that you made,
so you should fucking flaunt 'em."
"You should take responsibility,
your human right and liberty,
your 2A gun privilege and end this shit."
"You're fucking worthless.
The scum of the Earth.
And if you weren't then you'd be happy, chap."
"Ha!
But look at you,
you're handicapped."
"Your heart's in the wrong place."
"There's evil running through your veins."
"You've made it a long way,
but you ain't gonna finish the day."

Now shut the fuck up!

But the mirror doesn't listen,
because I'm trapped inside my head,
and now the room is spinning...
I think it's time I make some new decisions.
I think it's time I make a life worth living.
I think it's time I find a wife and settle down,
but I'm still drowning in my doubt,
that I'm not better off
six feet down in the ground.

How can I be loved?
How can I become somebody's "someone,"
when I'm strung out, come undone?
How come they can't see me
as I view myself?
I'm bleeding out.
I'm searching for the answers,
but I'm deafened by the sound
that our social climate amplifies...

But maybe I'm too close to this.

I'm looking for perfection,
but I'm not convinced per-*fect* exists.
Not anymore.
But maybe that's a strength of mine.
Maybe that's a lesson that I had to learn with time.
Maybe that's the key to happiness,
the understanding that
there's darkness so you see the light,
you just have to bear the fucking punches.

But in the midst of that,
you need to find a love for something
that will help you turn the corners,
so you don't get lost exploring
through this life with no direction,
only finding fruitless squander.

Because you're better than that.

Everyone is better than that.
But we do this to ourselves,
and then we wonder where salvation's at...
Fucker, *it's you.*
No one else will do it for you.
God damn, use YOUR moral compass.
Guide yourself out of this darkness,
and work hard, every day.
Because your value's paid with labor,
and your purpose with the cross you bear.

So put that weight up on your shoulders,
despite how hard,
because you'll make it there.
Because you're stronger every day,
if you survive and keep your health right.
And one day,
you'll be an old man,
enjoying the *-richness-* of his life.

Be Better

"No...
I don't know
the things you know,
but still I'm better off."

Which is something that I tell myself
so I don't get involved.
Because I don't like the odds
of *this thing* working out between us.
I'd rather be by myself
finding solace in my *genius.*

Wait...
I'm dumb as fuck.
Cashing in on luck,
'cause I ain't learned enough.
I'm young and dumb with nothing
but a couple of thoughts.
A couple lessons from the battles I've fought.

"But that ain't shit, kid.
Quit acting like a slick prick,
who will, "be alright."
Because life will kick you in the ass
if you don't act right."

And I know that,
but I'm stubborn.

I don't even, fucking, listen to myself.
So how the hell am I supposed to
hear the answers to these prayers,
if I don't even fucking ask 'em?
I ain't ready to hear it.

But I'm still ready to jump
when it comes to spouting opinions,
like I've got wisdom somehow past my years.
Like somehow I don't fear
the other side of life.
If anything, I egg it on.
I'm begging for it.
Please just end me now.
But there I go again,
acting like I'm smart.
Acting like I know what's good for me.

*"You may as well just quit before you start,
there's no one noticing."*

Because there's no one there,
and that's exactly what I wanted.
But be careful what you wish for,
'cause one day you'll have to own it.
And one day you'll finally know
that other people make you stronger.
But when you're left alone
you'll realize that
you should have been better.

So how the hell am I supposed to hear the *answers to these prayers,* if I don't even fucking as 'em? I ain't *ready* to hear it.

I just want to fly. I just want to fly.

I Just Want to Fly

I just want to fly.
But because now I'm used to smoking,
I ain't feeling high.
I think I've plateaued.
I ain't even feeling fine.
This is my new norm.
Space and time are being misaligned.
I'm taking stock in new form,
in search of heaven or sublime inclination
to change my state of mind.
My soul is starvation,
can't feed its appetite.
A sign of our nation.
I've been produced by this.
I've been seduced by the thought of cash
in its fluid state,
'cause I've been dealing in fool's gold
from my foolish take.
I'm... getting tired of being wired,
but I fire up.
I'm... getting tired of base desire,
but I fuck 'em.
I'm... I'm worth the life that I've lived.
I've built a heart that can give,
maybe two fucks,
then I'm out of it.
I'm honest,

but, life is really something.
I can't unsee shit.
I can't un-dream a vision of *heaven*.
I think I'm in it.
I've been lost,
but I've been tapping into *something*,
seeing stars throughout the day
when I've been dreaming up
which scheme will bring freedom.
I'm...
In desperate need of it.
I need this weed to hit.
I'm feeling anxious,
like nothing else here could save me.
It's...
A lot to take in,
but I'm doing alright.
I'm still alive for the moment.
I guess it's sacred time,
but I just want to fly.

But because now I'm used to smoking,
I ain't feeling high.
I think I've plateaued,
I ain't even feeling fine.
This is my new norm.
Space and time are being misaligned.
I'm taking stock in new form,
in search of heaven or sublime inclination

to change the pace
of this race of life that I'm facing.
I'm...
I'm getting older.
The summer's hot.
I prefer the cold,
and I just really need to slow things down.
I need a day off.
I need to take a breath of life,
and maybe let God say something.
I've been too busy to hear it.
I've been too busy running fearful,
delving deep in experience.
I've been too caught up in my daze,
whether day or night.
Fuck it.
Maybe I'm crazy.
I...
I know everything,
but nothing at all.
Am I out of mind?
Maybe soon I'll see my time has come.
Maybe soon...
I'll be tapping on heaven's door,
but their sign is off—
and they won't let me in.
"You did this to yourself."
They'll all be singing their shit.
"You didn't believe us."

"I guess you weren't enough."
"Yeah, you tried to lead a life of love,
but never gave your life to God."
"So fuck off."
And I just...
I just...
I just want to fly.

But because now I'm used to smoking,
I ain't feeling high.
I think I've plateaued,
I ain't even feeling fine.
This is my new norm.
Space and time are being misaligned.
I'm taking stock in new form,
in search of heaven or sublime inclination
to change my state of mind.
'Cause fuck, I'm impatient,
and fuck me, I hate it.
Because I've been sitting 'round,
just waiting to die.

I Need to Get Right

I've been smoking all the time,

and now my lungs have been fucked up.

But what did I expect?

I've been drinking and eating in excess,

every day,

and this here's what you'll get.

Don't be surprised about it.

I've made my life around this.

And I did it with the knowledge of the pain,

causing inflammation,

acid ripping, burning through my veins.

'Cause I don't give a fuck.

Or I used to not.

Because now I know I need to fucking change

or I'll begin to rot.

Because I guess I care now.

I'd rather live.

Why not take the chance?

And I could do it as I've done it,

but it probably wouldn't last.

I need to get right.

But... I need to smoke to sleep at night,

and I drink to add a spin.

Because you can walk the straight and narrow,

but it's *fun* with added risk.

But this "fun" here has been killing me.

I'm getting close to my limits.

And I've been thinking of the times
I've nearly died,
but stayed with it,
and how I had never felt alive before.
I want more of it.
More than this.
More starry nights with *wondered bliss.*
More air to breathe, fresh, mountain crisp.
More pain with brewing anger,
so I'll find a way to deal with it.
Give me the good. *I want the bad,*
because I might need the experience.
I might need the thickened skin
to battle off the delirium
that this world's been stricken with.
What many people coin as sin.
What has led to many, countless deaths.
Whatever statistic I'll be in,
I need to get right.
Fuck,
how much do I need to change?
What all does it take to be a good man?
I've never known.
This day and age keeps on complaining
about everything that makes me who I am.
So how the fuck
am I supposed to heal these wounds?
They're already singed.
I need to get right.

I want more of it.
More than this.
More starry nights
with wondered bliss.

...Every now and THEN I GET a glimpse or hint of A REMINDING MEMORY me of dreams WHEN I was YOUNG. When imagination, light free, WOULD lead to GOOD and FUN. How I USED to see the WORLD and what I've lost as I HAVE grown. I MISS THAT sunrise...

The Haze

...Every now and then
I get a glimpse or hint of sun.
A memory reminding me
of dreams when I was young.
When imagination, light and free,
would lead to good and fun.
How I used to see the world,
and what I've lost as I have grown.
I miss that sunrise...

Obviously, I had built up some pretty substantial barriers in my heart, mortared by hurt and frustration. I think they developed as a form of self-protection, despite how deeply destructive they were. But breaking those barriers back down, once they were there, took quite some time. Particularly because of how resistant to change I had become. The best thing I ever did, though, was to begin surrendering to my own healing. If you have found yourself in a similar position, I hope those words sink in; *surrender to it*. You will save yourself a lot of grief if you do.

The funny thing is, we often know exactly what needs changing in our lives, but choose to do the opposite. I have seen this a lot. Maybe it's our intuition or a sixth sense. I'm not sure. But it can be screaming at us, and in all likelihood we'll end up making excuses for our bad behavior instead. I am absolutely guilty of this. *You might be too.* I would be willing to bet that everyone does this in one way or another. The quicker you can get a handle on that, though, the better. Because you will never be able to fully heal from *any* of your problems until you take some accountability for the role that you're *likely* playing in them.

That idea might seem a bit harsh or off-base at first glance. Because how could you be responsible for the pain that others have caused you, or that the world has thrust upon your shoulders? But I promise you, if you're still holding onto things months or years down the line, it's probably true. Not to say that the actions of others are your fault. They aren't.

You can't control the will of anyone else. However, how you have responded or allowed those things to affect you, is your responsibility and yours alone. Accepting that can be tough, but once you do, it very well could be the thing that sets you free. Because an honest admittance of what is being clung to, is the same realization of what can also be let go.

Immediate hurt in response to circumstance is normal. Anything beyond that, though, can be unhealthy and may need to be addressed. Be careful not to take on *blame,* though. That can cause you to spiral down into a cycle of negative thoughts or self-deprecation. *Reel those things in.* It isn't necessary to punish yourself for things that you have likely already suffered. What's important is that you understand that *your reactions are yours to control,* and in order to feel different, you have to react differently. You absolutely have the ability to rewrite the narrative that plays over and over in your head. I am living proof of this. All it really takes, ultimately, is a deliberate focus on your well-being and an unwavering desire to heal. You might first have to overcome any addictions that may have formed in regards to your heartache though.

If you notice any resistance in yourself to that statement, just hear me out. How is it that you could be addicted to your pain? Nobody ever wants to feel that way, right? *But you might be actually.* Anything can become addictive if it serves you, in any capacity, even depression and anxiety. Especially if it's coupled with substance abuse. However, even when it's not, people can easily derive an odd sense of significance from their sadness or stress.

Particularly if others begin to coddle them and offer extra attention and support. If you don't think that attention can be addictive, you are fooling yourself. *It absolutely can.*

In my case, like many others, I opted to "escape" as my method of self-soothing, often with alcohol, weed, and women. I didn't fuck around too, *too* much, but it was definitely enough to become destructive. Escaping is where I really went wrong, though, and is ultimately what did the most damage to me. Because in the end, it only left me heavily addicted across the board, *living in total misalignment,* while still not having dealt with any of my problems.

The tricky thing about addiction, which I have learned, is that even though the drug or bad habit may feel like an escape, it is actually making the underlying problems worse. Your troubles get put on a pedestal in your mind, bringing them to the forefront and amplifying them in order to justify another fix. It's a pattern of addiction I have heard of, but don't hear talked about enough.

From experience, I will tell you that it always seems very reasonable to try to shut your problems down in this way, because it's *easier* than actually dealing with them. Unfortunately, though, what happens is that your brain begins to wire circuits between the pain of your troubles and the relief that you find in your drug of choice. So when the time comes that you're inevitably dependent on them *and your body needs a hit,* your troubles become the only thing that occupy your mind. Leaving you convinced that these issues are ever present in your life and are much worse than they might actually be.

Sadly, the end point of this path is that the good things in your life turn up next on the chopping block of justification. Until one day, you'll either catch on to the ruse and break the spell that you're under, or have destroyed enough of yourself that you stop breathing. I have either seen or lived it all, smoking and drinking myself into asthma and bad health, and breaking up nearly every relationship I had developed because of it. I always kept my circle pretty small anyway, but as the patterned remnants of my past spilled over into my present, and the chickens came to roost, I ran from even them. We were really all the same though, *some even worse than me.* But we played off of each other like bad tunes, with the drugs surely aggravating the issues; alcohol in particular, which is one of the worst there is.

It's an unfortunate reality that many people never find their way out of. Rarely for the lack of trying, however. Overcoming addictions is remarkably difficult, and it can drive you crazy if you're not careful. *Temptations can be powerful.* That is why getting to the root of your problems first is so incredibly important. Otherwise, you'll just fall back into your mistakes, and what you're trying to unwind will leave you in a tangled mess. *What you're combating in your heart needs to be made clear.*

It's not an easy process, and I have been far from perfect on my own. It is definitely worth the time spent, though, because you get your life back, *or at least the joy of it.* This section, *The Haze,* may not describe it perfectly, but it's a jumbled mix of thoughts from that time, as I started to figure it all out. Hopefully I have captured the anxiety.

Little Pond

What do we do
if these ripples turn to waves?
If these trees
all come crashing down,
or rocks slide out of place?
I think I dream too much.
This is just a little pond.
I should find peace, or something.
I'm way too trapped in my head.

I'M way too
trapped
in my **HEAD.**

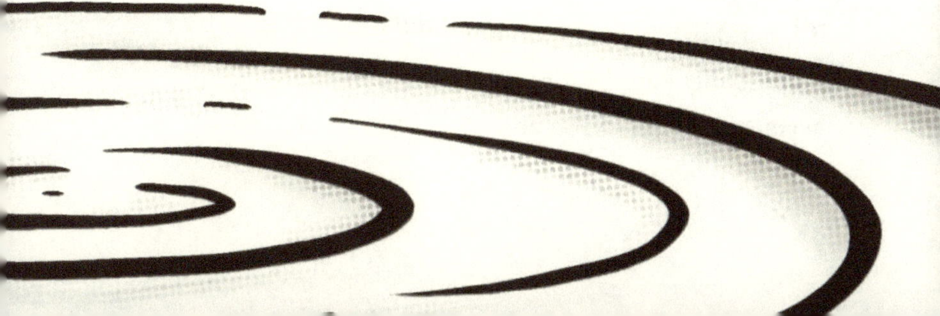

What Do I Want?

I want there to be a challenge,
but I also don't want to deal with it.
I have two conflicting thoughts at the same time.
I don't want to hear them,
but I don't want to fall victim to either.

So,
I've been *chillin'* within the margins
with my vision left unclear.
With a walk of bitter cadence,
and a constant dream of next year.
Next month.
Next hour.
Next thought.
Next unhinged, filtered fear.
Next moment of this "reality,"
forgetting
that I'm still standing here.
Frozen by these cunning thoughts,
but do they want what's good for me?
Is there passion for finding truth,
or am I lusting for eternity?

Honestly,
if I could live forever
I'd probably end it soon,
because I don't see the point.

It's the fact that I will die
that brings a value to my life.
I'm a minted,
one take,
limited edition,
who's still coping with the idea of death,
but I think I've got a grip on it.
The problem is this life to live.
The issue's my next breath,
because I'm betting that I'll smoke with it.
I'm starting to understand
that there's a pattern to my madness
and a method to my greed.
It's got a message.

"Just keep feeding till you bleed,
never concede,
because even that is not enough.
I want it all,
so give it to me."

But I don't want to take it from you.
I don't want to steal.
What I have needs to be earned
or my success was never real,
and that's the challenge.
But it's daunting...
And I just don't want to deal with it.

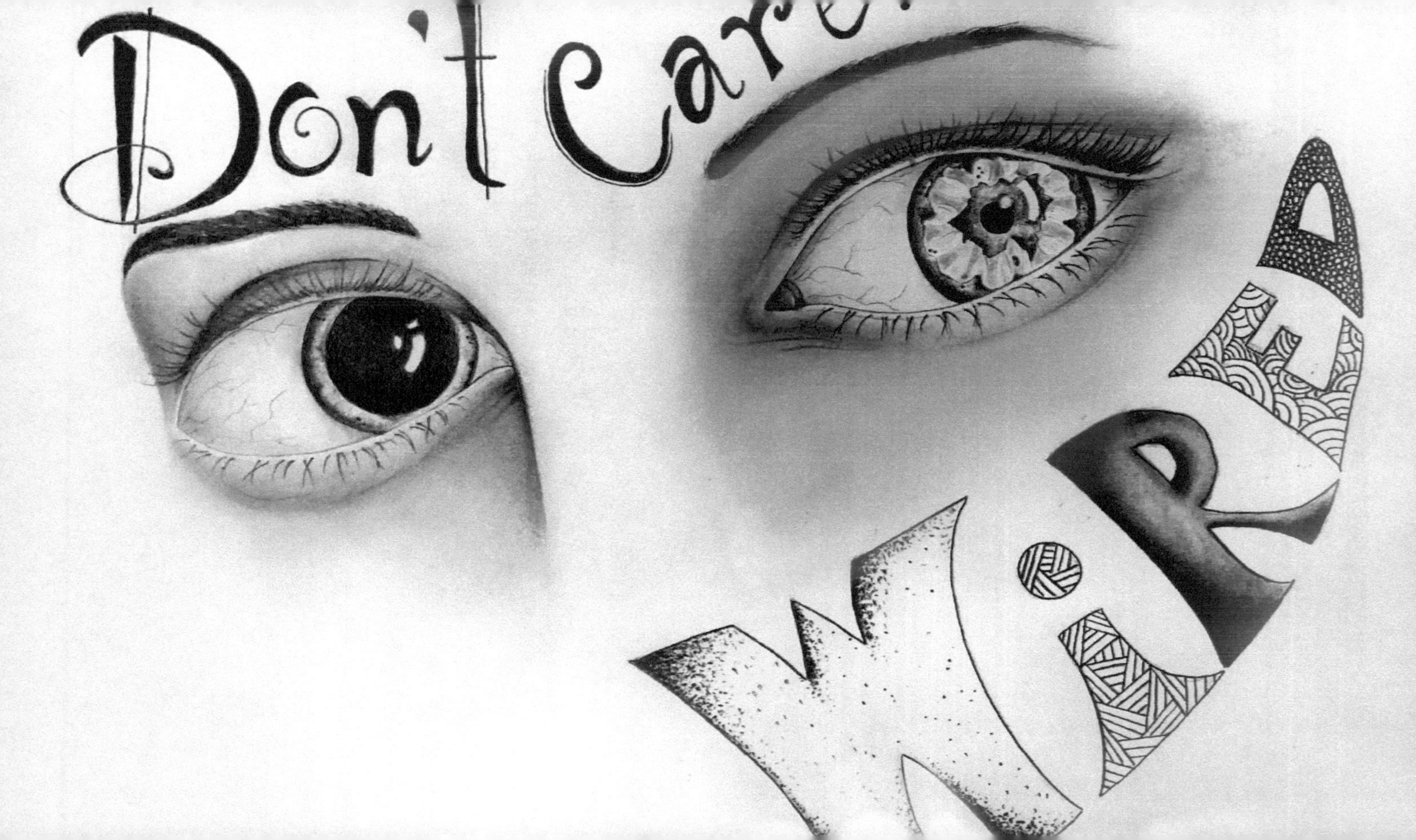

Don't Care.
WIRED

Addict

Do I want to get better?
That's something I have to think about.
This life that I'm living hasn't been so bad,
but that might be my addictions talking.
They don't like change.

Stitched

I feel like I'm the baddest, good guy.
I feel like I'm the *finest* piece of shit.
Over time I've learned to know myself,
and over time *I've noticed it.*

I'm good at what I do,
but I'm always falling short.
Never meeting *my* expectations.
Always wanting to change,
but never knowing where to start.
I just keep wandering.

I just keep wondering,
that if I remain the same today
will this *life thing* here be squandered?
It's a lot to take in,
because the answer's pretty clear.
But out of fear
I just don't hear it,
or I steer the conversation
pretending I didn't listen.
Because even though I need it,
I don't want the criticism.
I just can't handle it.

Maybe that means I'm weak.
Maybe that means I'm soft.

Maybe that means I won't amount to much,
and maybe I'd be better *lost*.
Because I just can't stand this shit.

But that's life,
and I could either die or take the hit,
and I guess I'd rather live
so give me the scars with wisdom's stitch,
and I'll learn to handle it.

But frankly, that's just the start.
If I truly want to thrive
or feel alive,
I've got to grow up.
I've got to be the man that I'll become.
Because tomorrow starts today,
and the song of life is better sung.
So, let me get to *singing*.

Let me get to aging with every breath,
and hopefully forming better opinions.
Which can't be all at once,
but I'm thinking
I can take this step.
Because...
I don't want to be the baddest, good guy.
I want to be me,
without the contempt.
Because, I just can't stand that shit.

Because, it breaks my heart,
every time the mirror sees
that I'm far from my potential,
but this bar's been set by me.
I think I've been my worst enemy.

I think I've been my worst enemy.
but this bar's been set by me.
that I'm far from my potential,
every time the mirror sees
Because, it breaks my heart,

"Remember That"

So... I think I'm losing touch.
I try to see the good that's all around me,
but, right now I think I'm blinded
by this feeling in my gut.
That's been telling me to run.
To break free,
and stay far from love.
Far from anybody I could trust.
Because lately...
Those numbers have been dwindling.
I'm burning every single bridge
that's led me this far,
because this destination's *shit*.
And I can't circle back around
if it's been blocked up at the start.
I'm just trying to keep myself
from *fucking up again*.
Because it breaks my heart,
every time the mirror sees
that I'm far from my potential,
but this bar's been set by me.
I think *I've* been my worst enemy,
by leaning on a crutch
made of whiskey, weed, and women.
I've been drowning in it.
Suffocating senses.
Lacking censorship.

I can't control myself.
So don't think I'm the victim.
I'm a drug-lusting, cynical sinner.
Who's been trying to make a home out of twigs,
and then getting pissed
'cause it won't hold through the winter.
Or weather any little storm,
'cause this security's fickle.
So no wonder I've been insecure.
Closing every door,
swearing that there's nothing more for me.
Sometimes I want to scream
and break into a million pieces.
But, fuck me.
Somehow I'm still a dreamer.
And even on the days where I wish
that I wouldn't wake up,
there's a piece of me that says,
"You've got this."
"Yeah, you're bull headed, but you've got to live."
"You've got to give yourself a chance
to be a better man.
A better lover.
Be a better friend to everyone around you."
"You owe it to them."
"But you owe it to yourself,
you still deserve it."
"You're just a person, and nobody's perfect."
"Remember that."
"Remember that."

But What Do I Know?

I've been drunker than I should have been,
and higher than worth worshipin'.
I've lost my mind and got it back
so many times, I'm running thin.

I'm losing focus,
patience,
like I've spent the fucks I had to give.
My body's weak.
My thoughts are raw.
I've ground the gears I thought should spin.

But now they're locked in place.
So I can't sleep, or dream, when *absent sin.*
My spirit's shaking.
Bones are breaking,
and I'm losing hope of finding *light within.*

Because I'm blind to truth or knowledge
from the past, because I can't commit
to dogma's rife in blood and greed
that have left the world war-torn and singed.

And operate today like they'll be
absent of all consequence.
But consequently,
times are changing.

Because, we've been free.
In part pretend.

So progress is slow,
but glimmers hope
that we won't cause our end...

But what do I know?

I've been living like the cash is spent.
It seems like life is precious,
but I've numbed out nearly every second.

Do I know a thing?
Or is the purpose of this life, the tension?
Maybe God is real
and I've just been too ill to comprehend it.

All I really know
is there's a lot I need to change.
But really so do most of us.
So who *really* knows?

This life is strange.

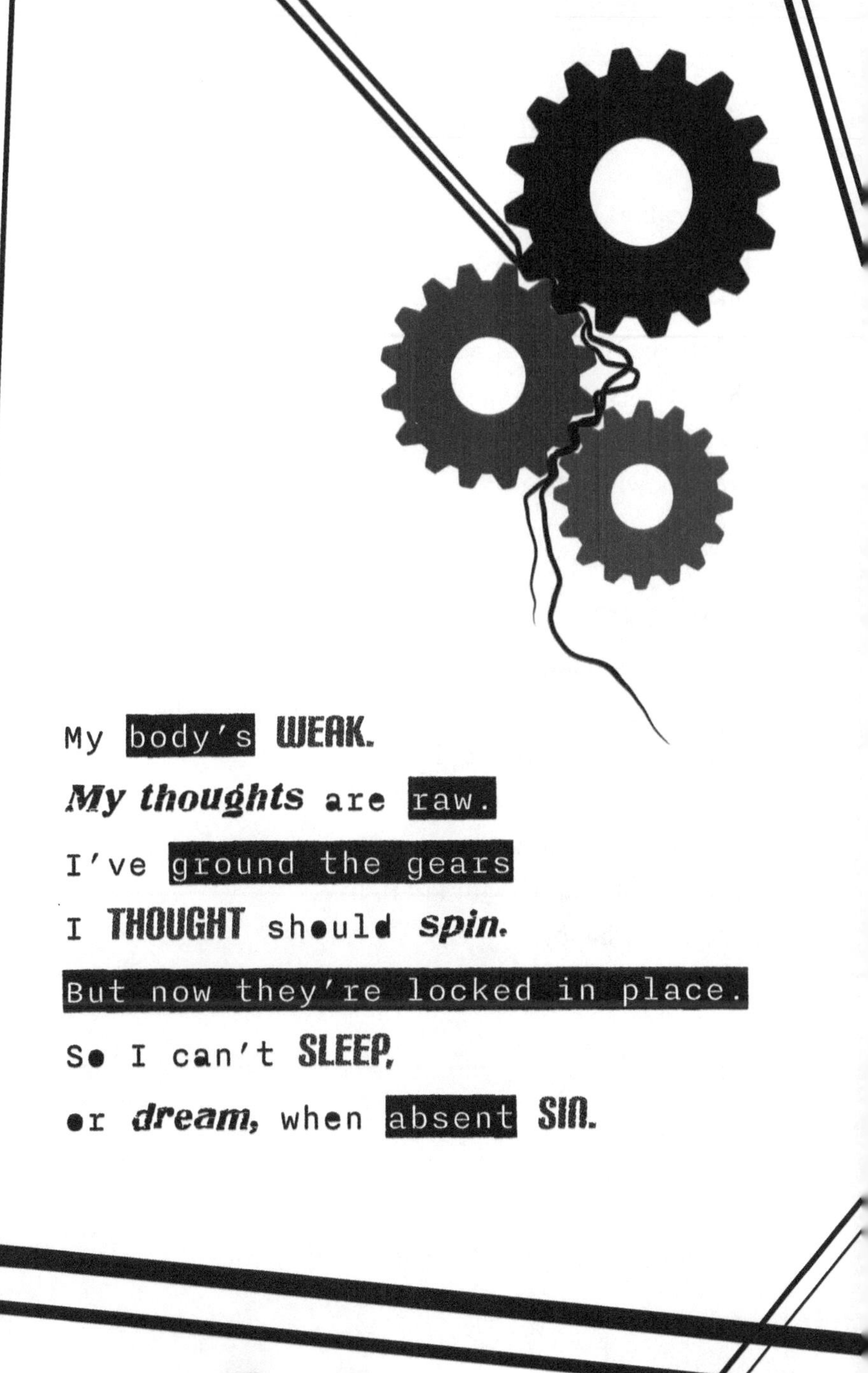
My body's WEAK.
My thoughts are raw.
I've ground the gears
I THOUGHT should spin.
But now they're locked in place.
So I can't SLEEP,
or dream, when absent SIN.

More Than Just a Moment

Sometimes I write fast,
but talk slow.
Sometimes I talk fast
while the thoughts are flowing.
Sometimes I never speak at all,
because I'm locked in thought.
With nowhere to go,
but down.

Nothing to do
but drown inside the sorrow
that this world provides.
Living on my borrowed time.
But maybe tomorrow
the sun might shine upon me.
Perhaps the stars might fall in line,
and I'll be happy,
for more than just a moment.

And maybe
I might write,
and talk,
and think,
about something more important, *than this.*

Am I Not Strong Enough?

Somehow
I've been convinced
that "I'm okay,"
but can't remember
being sober.

On and on for years,
can't go a day here
without smoking.

My liver "needs" a whiskey binge.
My smile "needs" a beer.
My mind "could use" some fucking weed
to drown out things it hears.

Because,
how come *it* should listen
to *my* crying out for help?
I've put myself in this position.
I should *get out* by myself.

Am I not strong enough?

LIFE
OBVIOUSLY
MEANS SOMETHING.
IF IT DIDN'T
THEN WHY ARE WE HERE?

What's the Point?

I don't know if everything happens for a reason. I mean, it feels like we are the ones who attach the "meaning" to things, *and then call it a good life*. Many people live happily that way, and maybe they're correct.

Life obviously means something. If it didn't then why are we here? I'm still trying to figure out its value though. When I look at the grand scheme of things, throughout all of eternity, my existence seems fairly insignificant. *But to me, it is everything.* To those I love and those who love me, my life is worth the world. In retrospect, though, the world is pretty small.

I'm sure many would say that the vastness of infinity shows the sure power and fury of God. But, what does that mean for me? How many worlds are out there? Does that potential for life inflate the markets dealing mine?

But, there's me adding meaning again, *like I know something*. Maybe there's no point to any of this, but something about that doesn't sit right. Perhaps I should meditate, or something.

Timekeeper

I'm not the clock.
I'm just the hand that's ticking by,
and I can't tell what time it is.

Seconds. Minutes. Hours.
All seem gone in an instant.
Like time has been devoured
by a lust for something infinite.

I feel like I've encountered, counter wisdom.

I fear these springs are winding up too tight,
but I never listen.
I'm just the ticking hand
who flickers,
bare of its significance.
Without a hand in saying how I go,
little makes a difference.

But I hope that time moves slow.
And although I'm not the one to tell it,
I hope someone is watching, reading,
clocked,
wise to what compels them.

Untitled

My fear is not strained, shallow breath.
My pain is not words said.
My worry is words left to speak,
when instead, I'll exhale death.
I sense my time might come too soon,
as if my angels hold my hand.
Walking me through life *let* left,
while I'm begging we might stand.
Quiet, still, just long enough
so my thoughts might find their end.
And that I might find the strength in me
to say what should still be said.
At this time, I know not what to speak,
although "love" rings through my head.
The same "love" once reminding me
not to die by my own hand.
And though I'll, surely, still misstep:
I should choose life *'til my day.*
But live beyond the shallow depths
of what will one day be my grave.
For now, there's heart yet left to sing,
and daylight left to see.
That even though words die as well,
while alive, those words should breathe.

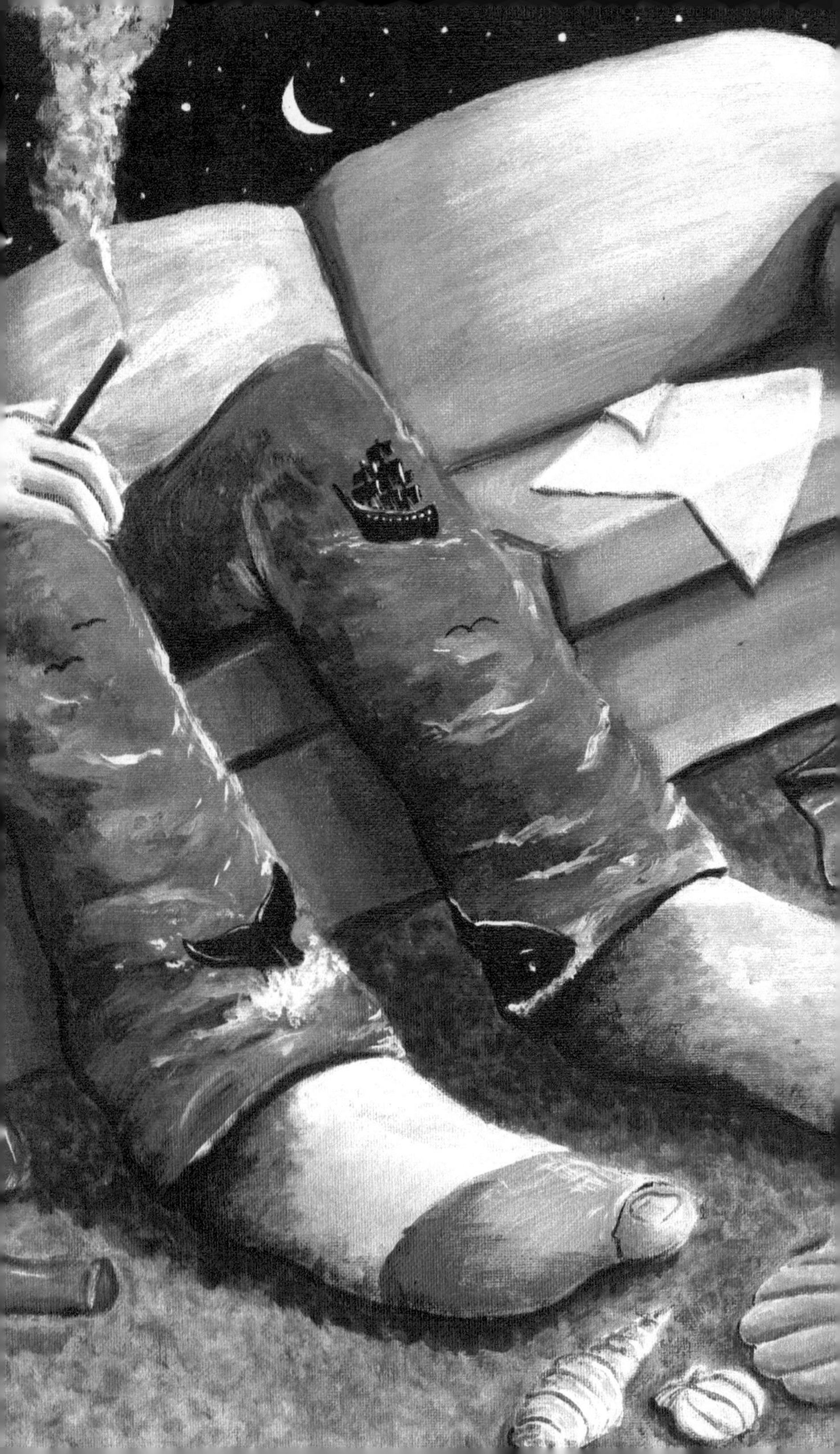

Twisted

I don't like to drink anymore.
I mean,
I still do it
but it's not the same.
I've been really high these days.
And with this twisted vision of myself
I think I'm okay.
I think my problems might just fade away.
I mean,
they're gone right now.
Maybe they'll stay
locked deep inside,
free from light,
out of fear that they might grow.

Because tangled webs of vine and thorn
can rightly trap a liquored soul.
Keeping taut the chaos,
struggle now with blood the pay-off,
or you'll sit there slowly wilting,
free from scars,
barely preserving what's been left of you.
Because, you're left scarred regardless
by its flagrant, ostentatious
ability to fuck you up.
Because now you know you're powerless,
your tissues growing weak.

At this point you've lost control,
and that just isn't who I want to be.
So, I smoke weed instead.

Which really isn't better,
because I can't control my head,
and shit,
if you're too lost in thought,
you may as well be gone and dead.
Because you're dead wrong
to think that you're worth *anything,*
high and on your couch,
past the point of falling out.
I just sit there dreaming.
Time wasted,
because you have to do things.
You have to make something of yourself,
or else your dreams will stay your dreams,
and your reality remains the same, damn thing,
that you've been trying to escape from.

But... still smoke a little bit.
Still drink on occasion.
It's okay to have escapes,
if you don't let them change you.

This Cell That I Call Home

Why is it that we live our lives in boxes?
Perhaps it's the easiest shape to build.
But, what is the price for living
in-between these cold,
barren walls?

Are we sacrificing chaos for order,
or freedom for boredom?
I think I ought to hang some art up.
Enough to, at least, distract me from
this cell that I call home.

I think we ought to be outside more.

In Time

I'm thinking one day I might grow up.
One day I might be the man
that I'm supposed to be, *or something.*
I'm still trying to comprehend
the difference between now and then,
and why it's taking so long.
But I can't figure out when that's supposed to be,
or when I'm grown.
Because, now my body's bigger,
but I'm still the same kid.
I just have a couple scars
to prove the life that I've lived,
but I'm not that different.
I've got a few more cracks and imperfections,
but my core is still glimmering.
I have some wrongs to right.
But I'm alive,
and there's still time to really live it.
So, I've been trying to find the time
to do some things that I love.
Because I don't think a man should sit
and wither like a stone.
I think I have to let my heart sing,
because I've spent enough time just dreaming.
It's time to turn *them* to reality.

Now my body's bigger,
but I'm **still** the same kid.
I just have a couple scars
to **prove the life** that I've **lived,**
but I'm not that different.

In Desperate Need of Truth.

What's the difference between you and me?
Us and them?
Black to white,
women to men?
Why do we have enemies,
and why do we have friends?
Why have hope for the future,
but fear for the end?
With love in our hearts,
but hate in our heads
we stumble around
and do it again.

Why?

Does it help us pass the time?
Is it just how we've evolved?
And does that make it right?

No.

I'm amazed we sleep at night.
Living how we've lived,
I swear there's nothing on our side.
And if there really is a God,
then, God damn, we're not enlightened.
I say that with my chest,

because I've seen what "He's" provided.
And, damn, I've seen how "He" divides us.
Because, really we're the same,
but yet the pious claim they're righteous.
And, the righteous rule the world,
because that's what a book decided.

Fuck that.

I swear, I'm tired of this bullshit.
Everyone's amazing.
Man, this world it needs a new print,
because this wasn't *made for us*.
We share the world and bear its pain,
just like everything on Earth,
no matter its fucking *fame*.

Damn.

SPIRIT

I have been searching for signs, and have gotten weird answers. It's tough to connect the dots, assuming there are any dots to connect at all. One of my biggest gripes with religion, or spirituality, is the vague nature of the thing.

I have been a big believer in the idea of coincidence, and have been quite atheist for some time now. But, I can't shake the feeling that there has to be a meaning to all of this. I have felt very nihilistic for a while, imagining that life is purely physical, and frankly nothing more than sheer luck; applying any meaning to simplistic interpretations of the brain functions that propagate our existence.

But I don't know. For a system like *us* to exist, that is striving to find meaning, there is a good chance that there is *something* that we are searching for. Some inherent truth that we are built to discover. It's too odd, really, that any of this is happening at all. There must be something there. *There must be.*

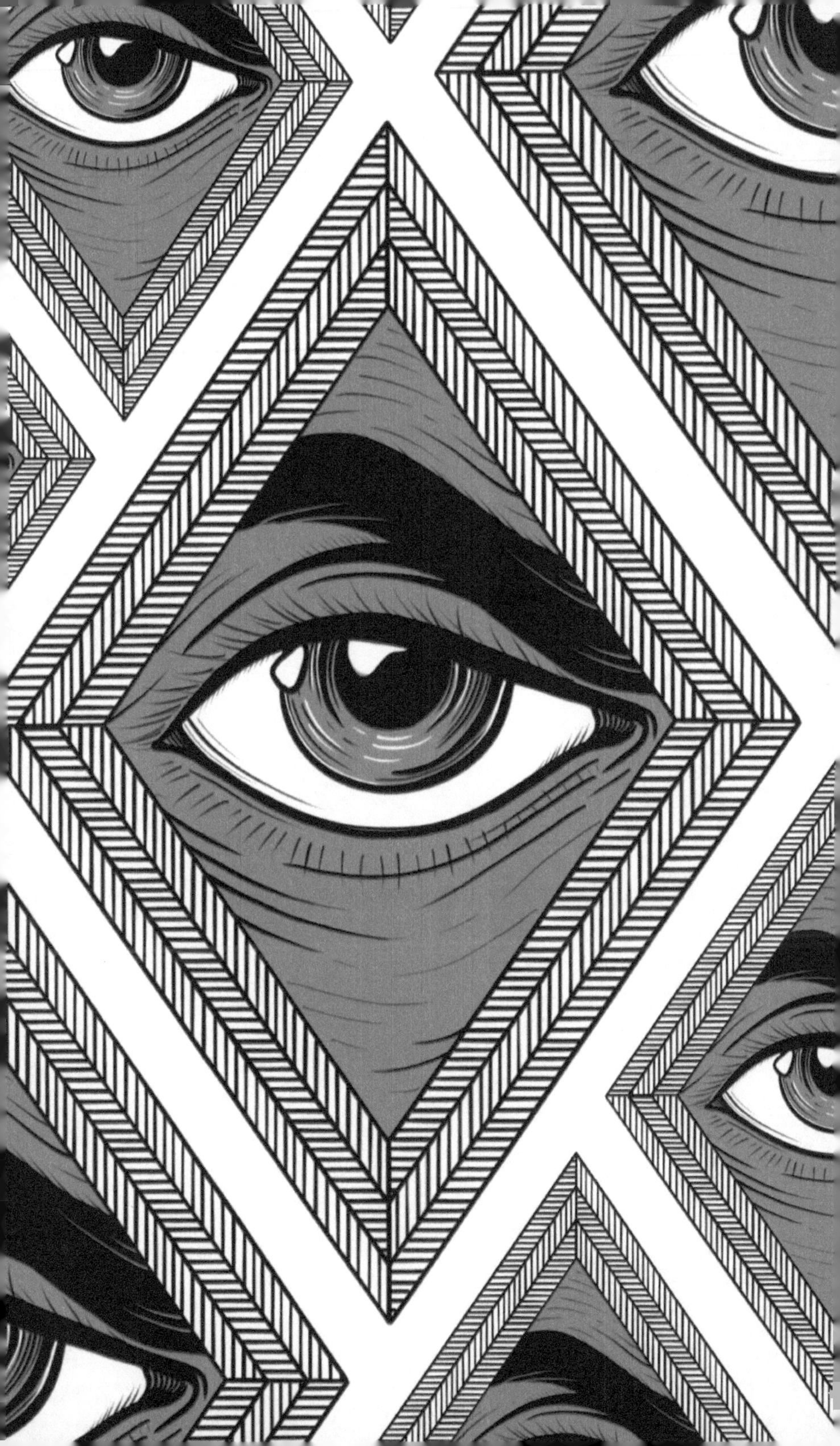

Just Keep Moving On

Some rooms matter more than others.
The ones where you shared your lives,
and maybe more.

It's hard to put on shoes
when you don't want to leave.
Because you know
that when you go,
this is what you'll always see
in your mind,
when you remember
your final look.

•••

You look in the mirror differently after love ends.
"What am I still worth to give to others?"

Hard to Love

After all,
we're all human, right?
Babbling on and on,
lashing out, causing fights.
Destroying what we love,
as if it's just to prove a point.
Then everything unfolds.
We're forced to live our separate lives,
but we're guarded by our pride,
because it helps us sleep at night.
It's helping keep me stable,
'cause I *know* this isn't right.
I just want to rewind.
Go back, but keep the time.
But I can't just let my mind
keep on running.
I'm shutting down.
I never thought that I would be me.
I guess I'm owning up to it.
I've got a couple problems.
I admit that I can't quit *this*.
I'm haunted by my past,
by my decisions.
It's really got me thinking.
Like, I could do better,
stay more committed.
But the truth is...

I'm a *victim* to my urges.
I'm caught up by *her* flirtin'.
These vixens they really work me.
Is it worth it?
These thoughts have felt xyresic,
and they're cutting to the core.
I really think I got the message.
Yet,
not much of me has really changed.
But writing all this down has
zapped some peace inside my brain.
I'm chillin'.

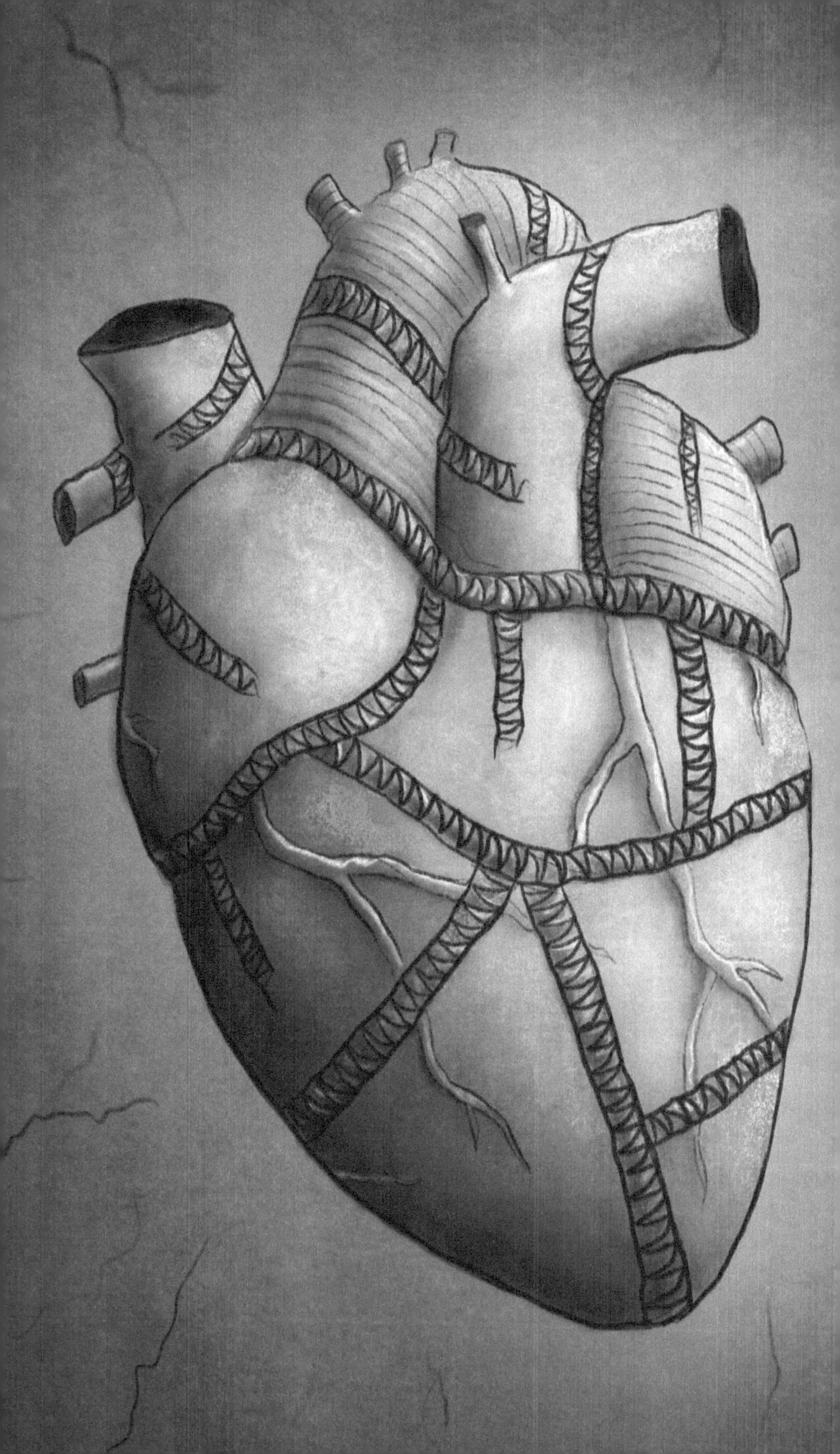

Patchwork

I liked to think
that nothing else
could ever phase me.
I liked to think
I'd seen enough.
This world is mad.
I liked to say,
"I'm reinforced
by every time gone crazy."
My chest was welded shut.
It weighed so much,
but I could stand.
I knew the world would hit me.
But I was safer now,
I hoped.
A thousand different pieces
made the "strength,"
I thought would hold.
I hoped to just detach,
take my wales
and bitter blows.
But as I sat back,
I watched my heart crash
and shatter like the shale.
I guess my patchwork's fragile.

Conflicted

"Love is what matters," right?
That's something I've been hearing my whole life,
and I've believed it.
I've built up expectations
with a dream of what it feels like,
and for the most part I've been wrong.
Which doesn't mean it's bad.
It's just different than I thought.
It's really more "responsibility."
Because tending to a heart
was never meant to be an easy thing.
You've both lived your lives apart,
and then one day, the two start melding.
Quickly turning into one,
that then the two of you are sharing,
and that is terrifying.
The thought that my life here is not my own.
The fact that someone else relies on me...
Am I grown enough for this?
When I barely know myself,
do I have enough love to give?
And if I give you all my heart,
will you commit the same, or up and split?
I've seen it all before
and now I'm hesitant.
I have trouble trusting folks.
Shit, I have trouble trusting me.

My heart's enthralled in rope and chains,
a tangled lock
that wound for free.
I'm sure I could get out,
but would that really be the better thing?
I've been conflicted.

Growing Pains

Sometimes I wonder,
did I really fall in love?
Or was I caught up by the drug?
She was my new addiction.
I think my heartbreak's just a symptom,
but it's playing with decisions.
It's got me feeling like the victim.
Realization: *I'm a hypocrite.*

But I was young and didn't notice it.
But now I'm older
and I realize, I was cold as shit.
I've got this weight I'm always rolling with.
I cannot trust myself anymore,
because I can't stop
fucking with these *whores.*

I guess my dad, *he taught me something,*
but I'm far from feeling love.
Like my heart has been unplugged,
but my thoughts won't stop their running.
I need a sedative to calm it,
just to sleep.
Fuck this yawning.

I really need the sun up,
because I'm better in the morning.
But the stargaze is coming,

and its got a message for ya', Kev.
Life is far from over.
But I'm falling,
lost control,
and... this air is getting thin.
I'm barely breathing
and I'm feeling it.
Lost my focus,
barely seeing shit,
but I'm still growing.

I've still got a lot to learn,
but I've got even more to give.
It's my life so I'm gon' live it.
This is it.
I hope you hear this.

I'm a better man because of you.

I'm still sorry for your pain,
but I'm just glad to see you've made it through.
I hope you know that I'm gon' make it too.
There's a road of pain ahead of me,
but love is real,
and that's the proof.
I just can't keep acting foolish.
That's the truth,
but what's a fool to do?
When he hates sleeping alone,
and then he thinks of you.

I've been resorting to old habits.
But it's that, that's got me damaged.
I'm amazed that I'm still standing
with my head high.
Sometimes I swear I'm not the good guy.
But there's still some silver lining
that's trapped deep, down in my soul.
That lifts the weight up off my shoulders.
I'm no longer feeling cold.
Then there's the kick-start of my heart,
and it's gon' beat until I'm old.
And that's a promise to myself,
it's not just shit that I was told.

Damn.
These growing pains are crazy,
but they're still the things that made me.
And although these times are hard,
no, I wouldn't change a *damn* thing.
Which has been a bitter pill to swallow.
But it really had to happen,
because I can't just sit and wallow.
And worry about the past,
because it's gone.
That's life.
It happened.
But my future is up to me,
as I'm writing these brand new chapters.

LOVE IS REAL
and that's the PROOF.
I JUST CAN'T keep acting foolish.
THAT'S THE TRUTH,
but what's a fool to do?

Be Free

Right now,
it feels like every day
I'm running out of sun.
Right now,
it feels like every place
I've been is running down.
So now, I'm trying to find a way,
to run and stay.
So I don't have to hear
these people say,
"Our time is up."

My time is now,
because I'm around to see it.
I'm on the ground, still breathing.
My heart's still beating
with a will to compete
for this share of life.
My share of time to be free.
Hoping with time,
maybe I'll see,
that you live the dream
and then one day you rest in peace.
Because that's the *truth* of things.

But every day keeps running out of sun.
And when I can't see the light

I don't feel right.
Because it feels like
the dark is surrounding me
from the ground up.

I'm feeling trapped.
I'm feeling tapped out.
My head's on a swivel,
about to throw my fucking back out.
This anxiety is stress provoking.
Omni-*potent*.
Fuck, I've had enough.
So I guess I'll rest my eyes for a minute,
and then let them open
when the sun is up.
The light and love,
the source of life
and God above.
I'm here to see you.

Wait,
I might have figured it out.
We might be *thinking*
to observe what's around.
Perhaps,
like human conduits
for motion and sound.
Like we're a
part of this system

that's been put together naturally,
by complex, *mattered* energy,
and now we're here to *see* it.

But,
don't put a grade on it.
I'm failing it out,
'cause I'm not carrying the legacy.
I'm falling apart.
But,
destruction's just a part of this.
I'm guessing darkness too.
I'm guessing life's just fucking reckless.
Shit, I'm fucking reckless too.
I guess that it's been fucking perfect, huh?

There must be more to this.
But what's the fucking point?
I'm thinking soon that I'll be bored of it.
But...
Tomorrow is a new day
with new light in shining rays.
And maybe then I'll learn its language,
and will hear what it's *been* saying,
"Be free."

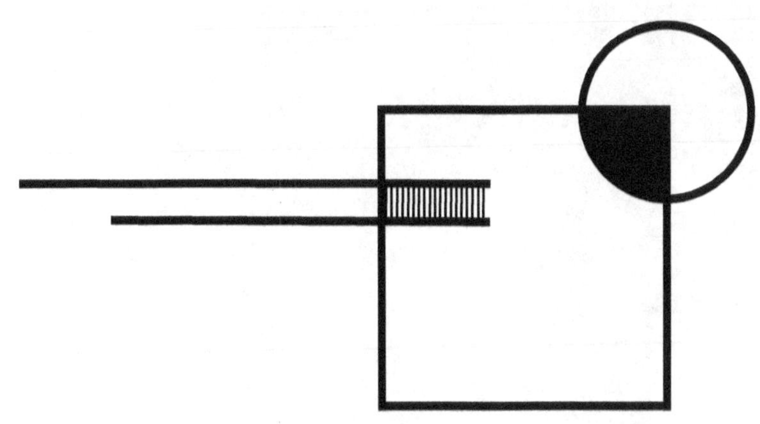

YOU LIVE THE DREAM
and then one day
YOU REST IN PEACE.

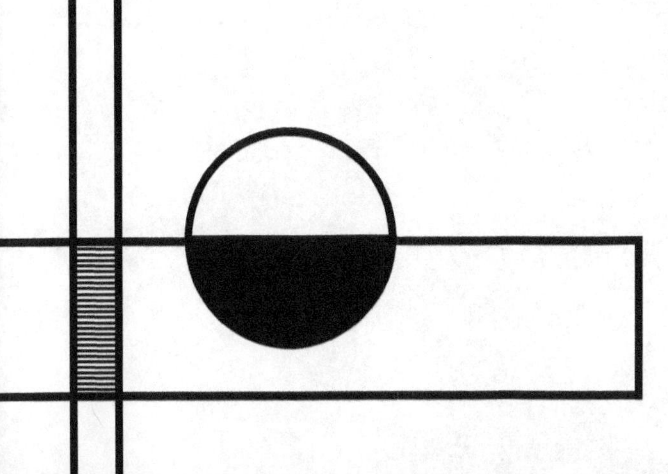

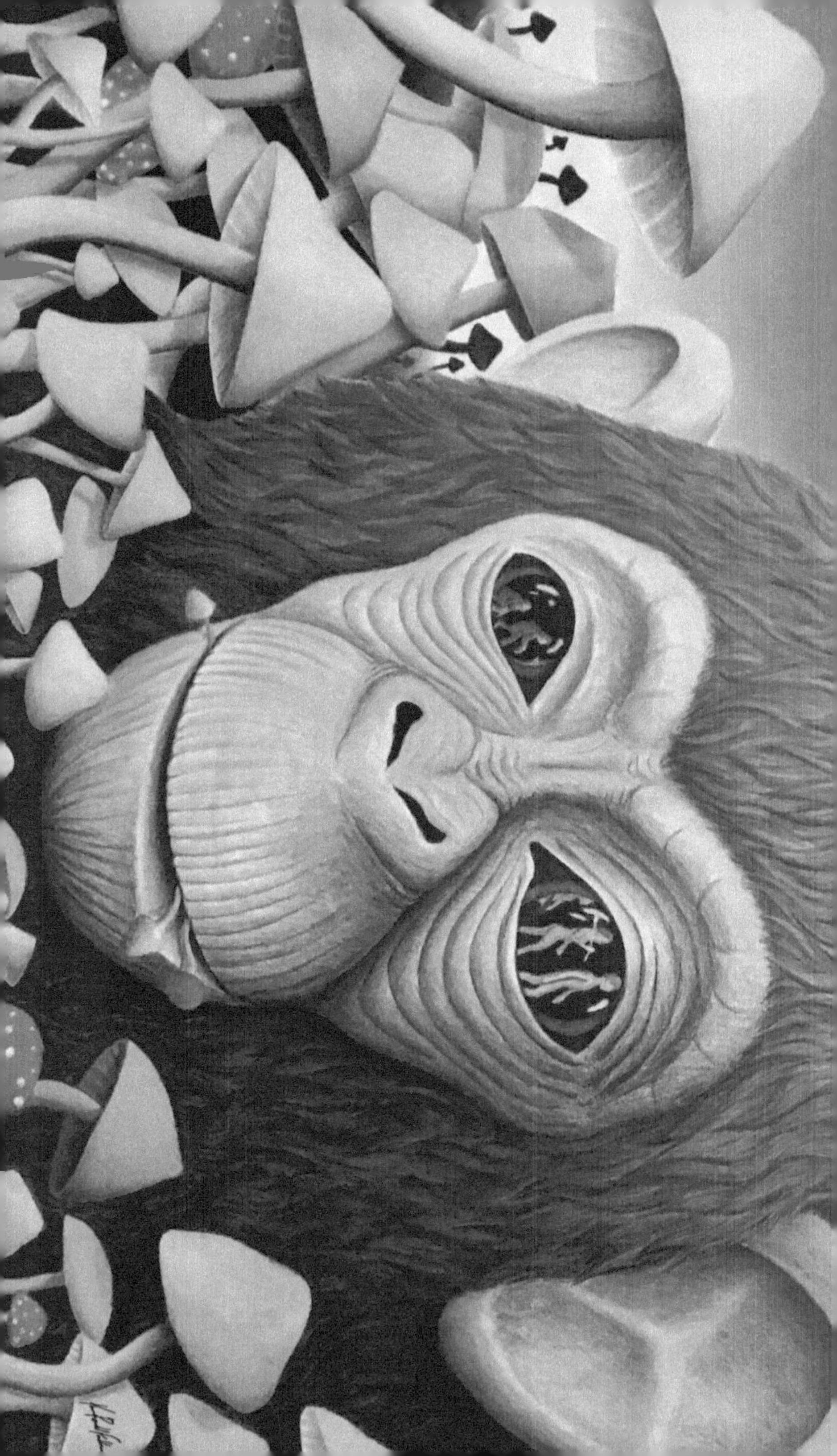

Psychedelics

Life is but a crashing wave of significance,
edging on the shore of something yet to come.

Sounds pretentious...
But you know what I mean.

It's a feeling.

Psychedelics
are in every way
what I have felt before.
Just maybe now,
it's everything all at once.

Truth

I would open my eyes wider if I could see more.
I would close them and keep them shut
if not just to dream.
I would learn to wield fire
to explore mount and shore.
But it's all fun and games
until the meadows burn.
Perhaps it's best to focus on keeping balance.

•••

Sometimes,
I think,
I had to think
that nothing had a purpose,
to realize just how stupid I've become.

Sparked

We are both

dull, daft
computing sacks
of ordered, balanced life,

and the light inside
that sets the thing aflame.

Worth Fighting For

I think I've seen my seventh sun.
I haven't slept at all.
I'd like to say this dream states fun,
but that tale would be too tall.

I could just exaggerate
and spin some words to sell it,
but that story's not the truth.
I'd have to lie in vain to tell it.

And right now, I'm strained enough
from taming my tempered blood,
and softening my hardened heart,
relearning what once was.

You'd think this would be easier.

ONE DAY

One day, I'll look back and grin.
One day, I'll find the truth in this.
One day, I'll read the words
between the lines,
secretly scripted.
The realities eluding me.
And I'll wonder why I ever stressed at all.

Right now, I may not see it.
Right now, things may seem plain.
But one day I'll understand all of this
and smile back, *without the pain.*

One day.

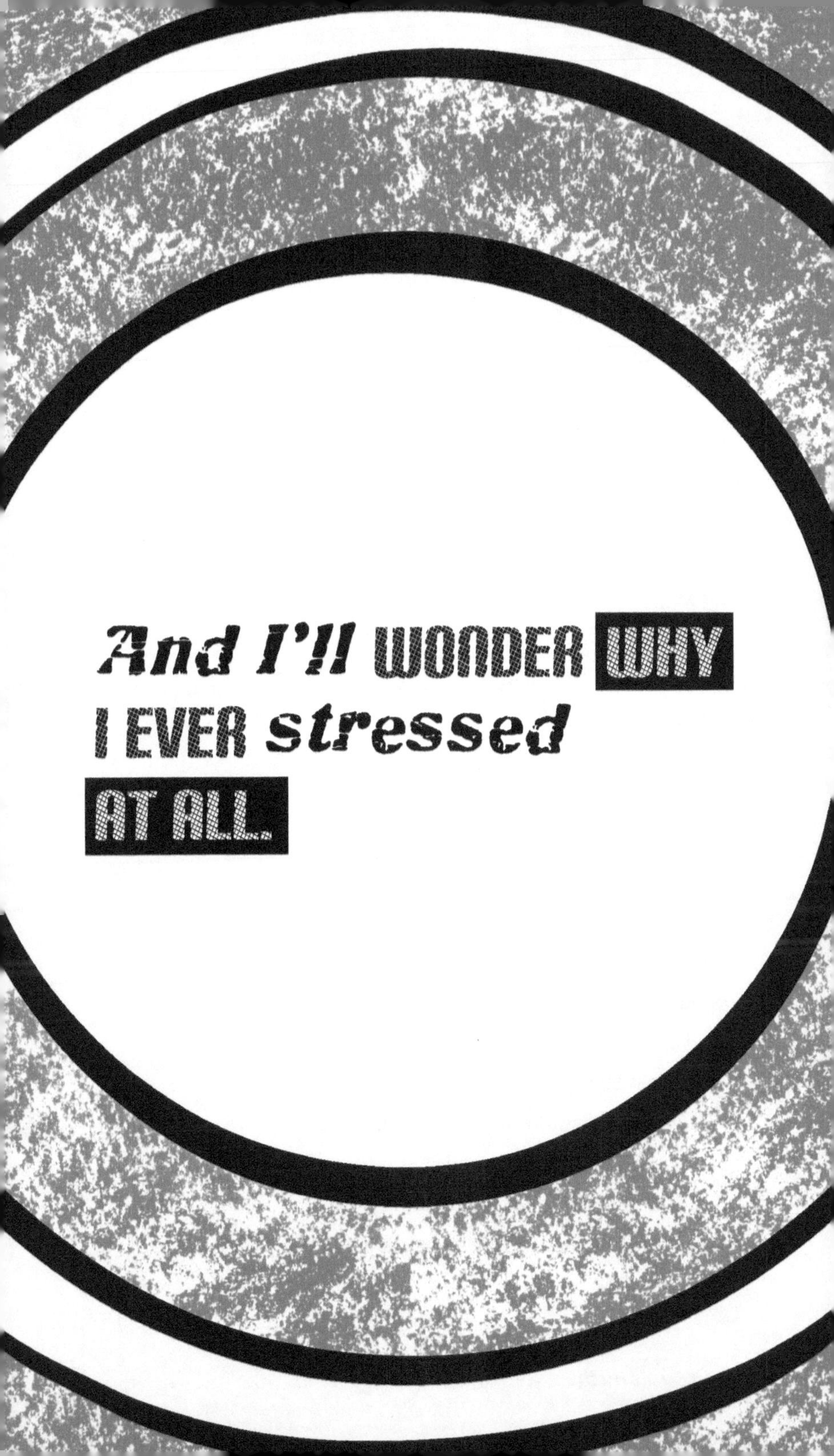

And I'll WONDER WHY
I EVER stressed
AT ALL.

I've Got This Life to Live

I need to quit being *sad.*
I need to let go of the past.
Because tomorrow's not today,
if you don't treat them the same.

I've got my life to live.

I don't want to waste
or give away
more precious time–
hating every moment,
or blaming the world
for dumb shit.

I've got this life to live.

I ought to be more grateful.
Because life,
although terrible,
is equal in its bliss.
And if you try to just escape
you'll never notice it.
Which would make it just as worthless
as I've thought or claimed it is.
But that's just a bad perspective,
and, frankly, opposite the evidence.

Life is worth the living,
and I plan to fucking live it.
It's a mix of good and bad,
because without bad
there isn't good experience.

So I guess I'll take it on the chin,
grow stronger from within,
and turn these moments into wisdom,
using them to learn to *grin*.

Because I've got this life to live.

I don't know why
I lust for shadows

The Sun

The sun is bright as hell,
but they're never bitter rays.
I'm thankful.
There's not a cloud in sight,
to hide the light of life.
I'm grateful.
But...
Somehow I'm still depressed.
Somehow I'm still convinced
I don't deserve this.
Like I'm better off in darkness.
I've been bitter.
Love is far-fetched.
But the sun's still shining on me.
I left my coat inside,
so I can feel the cold.
But the sunlight warms my heart.
I don't know why I lust for shadows.
I guess it proves
a world of depth
beyond my shallow, ill contempt.
Because I can't escape reality.
It's the light that makes the shade,
and it's our lives that highlight death.
And though the good die young,
I hope I'll live forever.
Or at least, long enough to see the day out.
Because the sun's still shining on me.

Some Fresh Air

It's a beautiful day. It's been a while since I have sat outside for no other purpose than just enjoying it. I should do this more often, even if just for a few minutes. I think that everyone might be spending too much of their time indoors. I know I have. Of course, we need to keep a shelter and home in order to protect ourselves from the world and its coming storms; but we are made of the world, *so maybe we should experience it.* It feels good to just be outside.

I find it funny how in art we will mimic nature and call it beautiful, when the real art *is* nature. Too often I choose to be locked inside, separated from it all. As an artist I am disappointed in myself. Because I have been thirsting for inspiration, but it's everywhere. I have just been choosing not to see it. *These clouds are fucking gorgeous.*

It's About Time

Lately I've been changing.
My inner self is fading.
Or... *the idea that I've had of me*
is different
and I'm contemplating,
who I've been and what I've done.
Like, what the fuck have I been thinking?
Who the fuck have I become?
I never thought I'd be this hated,
by myself.
My one true friend,
whose judgment now is slated.
Who's been with me through thick and thin,
but now has left me to this isolation.
To let me bear this world alone
with it's troubles, pains, and anguish
that have weighed me down for far too long,
and influenced the type of language
that has played in loops inside my head.

"You're worthless, foolish, tainted."
"You're nothing more than a stupid kid."
"You're average, weak, and jaded."

But, my time alone has let things still.
Those thoughts are less pervasive.
I'm growing to love myself again,

and have learned
it was my weakness that has faded.
My older self,
what I thought was me,
was parasitic and persuasive.
And had latched hooks deep inside myself
under guise of soft embraces.
Only tearing me down, furthermore,
until I was empty, lost, and faceless.
And amnesiac to my inner worth,
like my time spent breathing's wasted.

But... that's just not true,
and I'm seeing now
that life is truly sacred.
And you may only get it once.
So live it proud,
with integrity, love, and patience.
Otherwise,
you'll just miss out
on this gift,
this love:
creation.

it was my
weakness
that has faded.

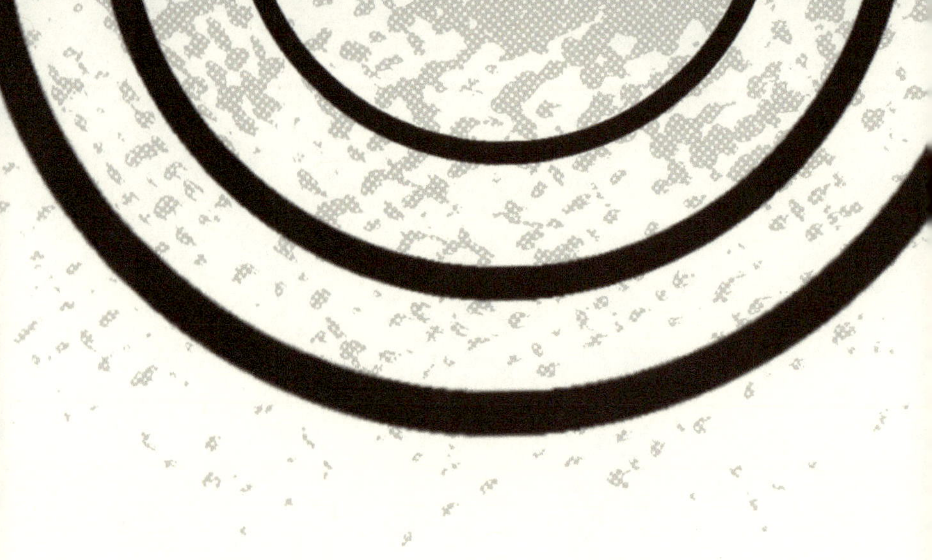

Like GOD
has something
to confide IN ME.

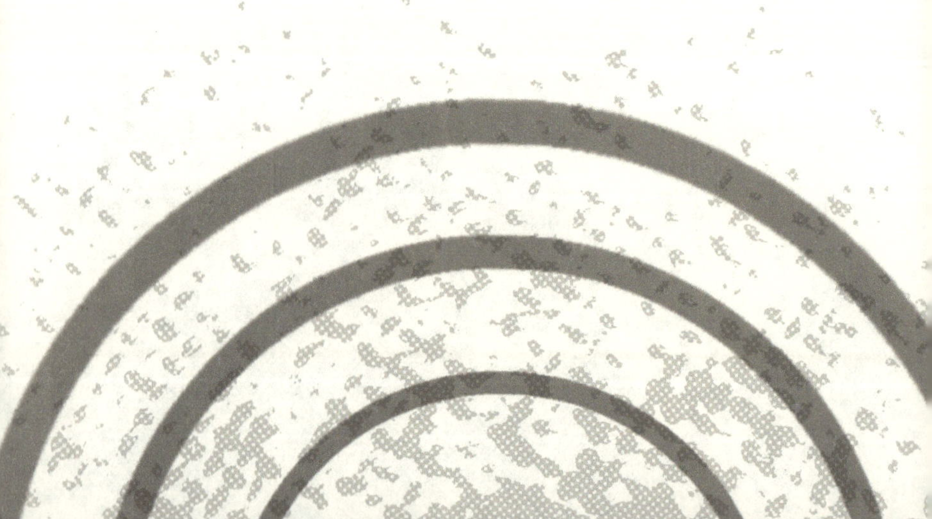

Call Me Sometime

Sometimes I think
that thoughts are there for finding.
Sometimes I think
that thoughts come, *finding me.*
Like God has something to confide in me.

Opportune

Sometimes the loudest love, won't speak.
Sometimes the strongest heart
will never get the chance to break.
And isn't that a shame,
that life keeps moving on…
Despite attempts to change,
or manifest things *better*?

To me,
sometimes it feels that way
with missed opportunity.
Those dreams that never played out.
That lived inside a wish,
but never had a chance or wish at all.
Maybe things have happened as they should.

Life is mostly good.

If I Die Today

If I die today,
tell my family that I love them.
Tell my mother she's a Queen,
and tell my siblings
to live in peace,
and not to stress about their brother.
Because,
I'm always going to be there.
I'm always going to care.
Even if my mind shuts off,
my love is in the air.
Because, *I'm part of you.*
You're part of me.
We're intertwined at birth.
And no, mom, she isn't perfect
but we're blessed that we were hers.
So, please, remember that.
I beg, I plead, I hope,
that you'll always have her back.
But I know you will.
Because I know your hearts are filled
with the love of life she gave to us,
and morals she instilled
at such a young age.
And while I'm proof that we can stray,
because life gets complicated,
poor decisions let you change.

And let you become who you'd hate to be—
you *can* become your worst enemy.
I learned that fucking lesson
when I saw just what the mirror sees.
I really wasn't happy
with potential, haunted dreams,
or with how this life was treating me,
but more so, *what I chose to see.*
It's up to you.
Your thoughts have power.
That's the truth.
And if there's one thing I could teach
it would be that.
Because,
what's in your mind
is what you do.
I pray it's good.
I want for each of you, the world.
And I wish you all the best,
so that your lives go as they should.
I love you.

Wonder

I wonder about things.
I wonder what you see.
I wonder what you think about.
I wonder what you dream.
I wonder how you view the world.
Is it the same as me?
I wonder.

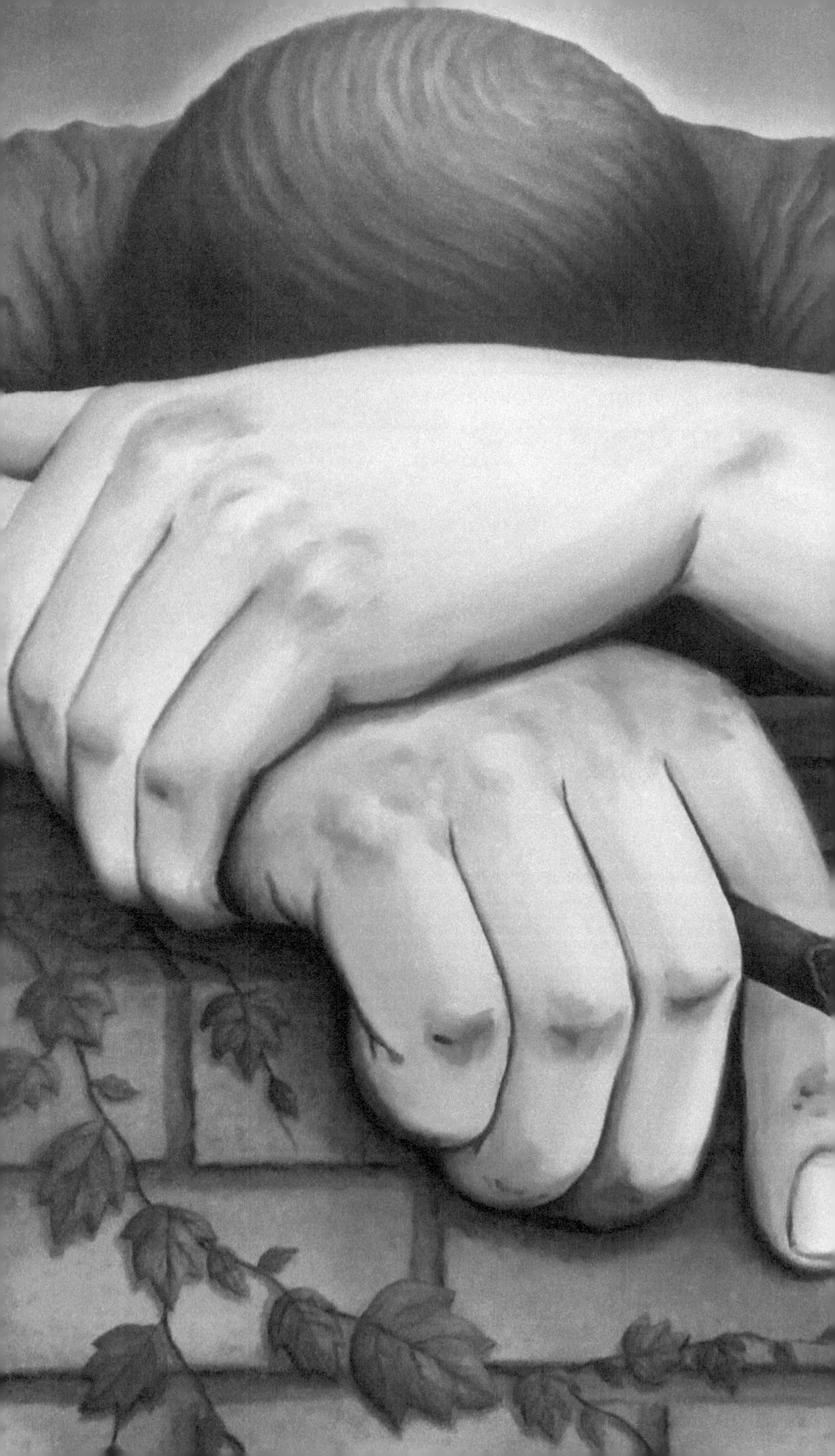

Here Comes More Rain

My knuckles bear the scars
of my frustrations.
My psyche bears a wisdom
much the same.
My world has been a whirl of wind
-If nothing else-
Cutting paths with rivers, rained.

Perhaps I should stay bitter;
grow deeper lines of scowling age.
Lose my sight to all things good,
as if all things fade the same.

But,
this search for *truth*
has led me far,
into the wild, free, untamed.
Where it's clear to see,
this is how things are,
and *this* they should remain.

For,
to be good,
there's bad.
To be peace,
there's war.
But to be free

there are *no* chains.
And I am free for now,
alive and well.
Still full of good,
though ripe with pain.

I am soon to let the wild bloom.
But first,
here comes more rain.

Don't Wait Any Longer

Go fast.

Go slow.

Go somewhere else than here.

Someplace where the stars will shine,

somewhere far from fear.

Go fast.

Go slow.

Move at any rate.

Just get the hell out of here.

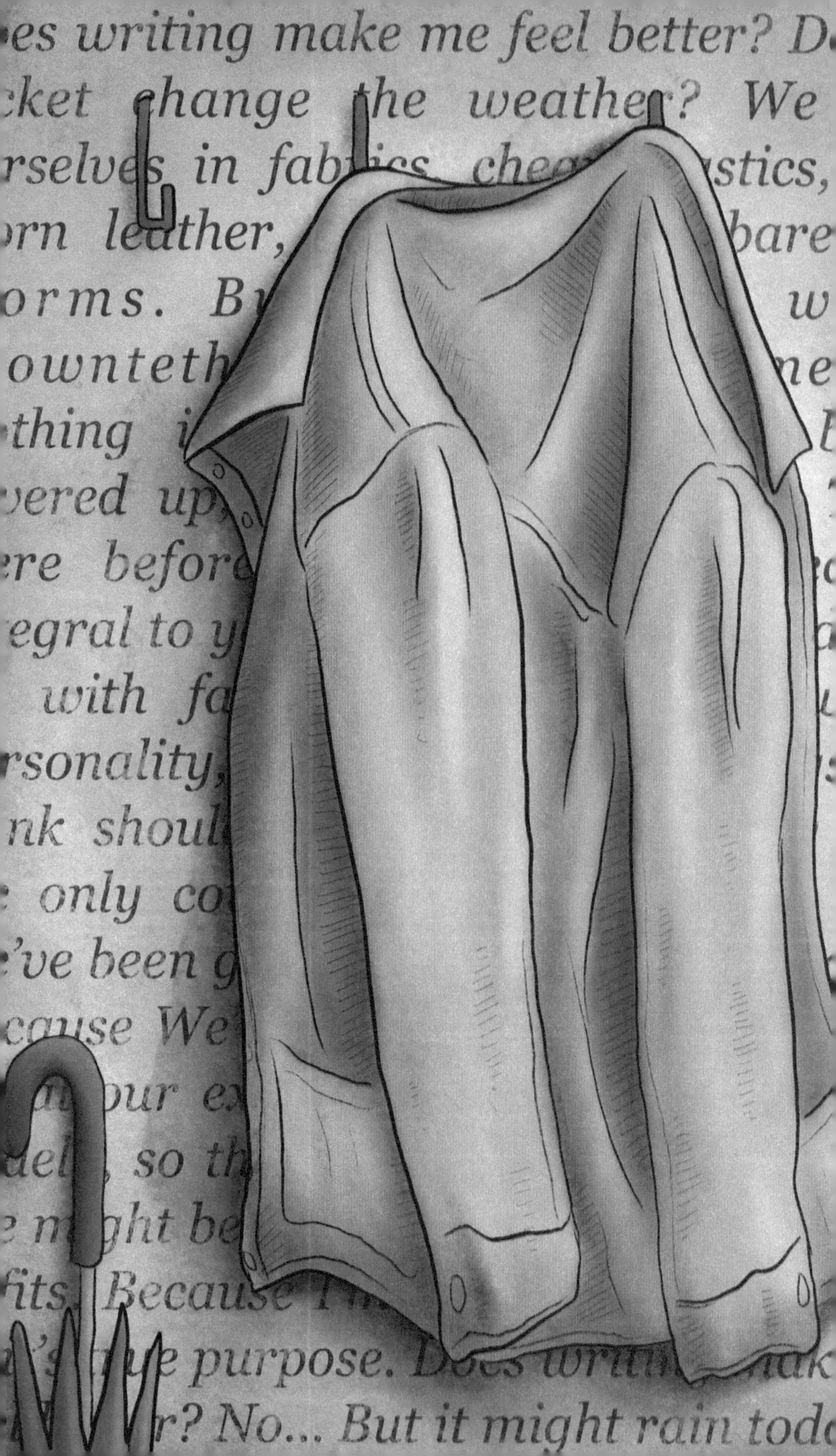

es writing make me feel better? D
cket change the weather? We
rselves in fabrics, chea   stics,
rn leather,   bare
orms. B   w
ownteth   ne
thing i
vered up,
re before
egral to y
with fa
rsonality,
nk shoul
only co
've been g
cause We
ur ex
del, so th
might be
fits. Because
's   purpose. Does writing mak
r? No... But it might rain tod

Cover

Does writing make me feel better?
Does a jacket change the weather?
We don ourselves in fabrics,
cheap plastics, and worn leather.
All in hope to bear our storms,
but as a people we've grown tethered to them.
Somehow clothing is the norm.
Somehow being covered up,
you're more yourself than were before.
Somehow cloth's become integral to your story.
Then we doll it up with fashion
to try and showcase personality,
but we hide the things we think should be unseen.
Forgetting that we only covered up
to warm our skin,
we've been getting lost in our appearance.
Because, we'd all like our garb
to *at least* equal our experience.
Display our status widely
so the world may rightly fear us.
We might be losing sight,
but I'll wear it if it fits.
Because I'm still in desperate need
of its true purpose.
Does writing make me feel better?
No...
But it might rain today.

Living Single

For a long time,
I loved being single.
I could do as I pleased,
and get pleased as I mingled.
And it was all in good fun,
but I felt my heart growing *evil*.
Because women became "objects" to me.
It's like their bodies matched
the harmonies my lust was singing,
and I couldn't get enough
of what that life was bringing.
Sure, I've always wanted love,
but, damn, I fought that feeling.
Shit, I'm still fighting it now.
It's got me lying low
just trying to figure me out.
I'm __ years old,
but still no better than a child.
I think it's time to be a man now.
But I've been lost and don't know how.
And I could say I never learned,
because my dad, he's not around.
But that's really no excuse,
because it's ME who brought the clouds
that soon covered up my judgment.
I had no sight.
I had no sound.

I was in a scary place.
I'm still amazed I didn't drown in it.
No, really I'm astounded.
I've been battling depression
while I'm smiling for the crowds.
But this is more than a confession
for the times I've acted out.
It's a promise to myself
that I'll *be better* starting now.
And I'm still single.
I've just turned myself around.
This time on purpose,
because love is really worth it.
In my past I've only flirted,
but me now,
I'm really searching.
Because my vision's looking clear,
and I'm prepared to look for years.
'Cause there's a woman out there for me,
and with her
I'll have no fear.
Cheers.

But I can't talk about love,
'cause I don't think that I deserve it.
I'm just another piece of shit
pretending that I'm worth it.

Yeah, I'm fucking great.

Do you believe me 'cause you heard it?
Or should I speak again,
so you can think of me as *perfect?*

Yeah, I'm fucking great.

Because *perception is reality.*
I hope my mom is proud of me.
I've tried to be my best,
but better's what I think I'll try to be.

'Cause I've been realizing
that I've been slippin',
and lately I'm feeling different.
It's been hard to keep my mind right.
I keep making bad decisions,
and I know that I'm to blame,
because I'm stubborn and resistant.
So my patterns haven't changed.
I've turned my habits to addictions.

So I'm getting high to cope with it.
I'm trying to see things clear,
'cause I've been caught up
by these loopy thoughts.
They're singing in my ear,
like, *"You're not worth it."*

Fuck.

"Who are you Kevin?
You don't deserve shit."

Fuck.

"Who are you hoping that you'll become?
Because you might just find a way,
but you're unstable so you'll break.
You've kept a smile that you've been faking,
knowing that's the only way
you're still alive today."

Shit,
I could've offed myself a week ago.
I'm battling depression.
It's a weakness that we never show.
Our world's about perception.
So, FUCK,
we don't want the world to know,
that we're in agony.
Because it's tough to hear,

and sad to see,
that someone you look up to
might have lost the will to fight their demons.
While questioning what they believe in,
and harboring a pain we know as Hell.
Losing love,
they once had for themselves.
I know this plagues a lot of you as well.

So what do we do?
Once our minds have been polluted
by these thoughts that leave us clueless,
because they won't just *shut the fuck up.*
They're way more than just a nuisance.
They're part of you.

It's the curse of being human.
Our brains are more advanced
than most of us know what to do with.
Which panders the idea
that maybe there's no real solution.
But...
Thinking in that way,
for me,
has only proven foolish.

The answer's love.

Which sounds short and sweet,
but, damn, it's tough.

It's more than we make stories of.
It's knowing that we really are the same,
and understanding, *everyone's in pain.*
Then taking time to try to make a change.
Because that might just save a life today.
A smile might keep a heart from breaking.
Acknowledging that, *"Yes, I see you too,"*
might be all it takes for *them* to make it through.
And might be all it takes
to turn *your* grays
to blue.
When all you see is black and white,
and lies outweigh your truths.
When you think you don't deserve to live
while caught in rotting feuds.
Search for love and spread it far.
You'll heal.
You'll be renewed.

No, your problems won't just disappear.
The journey's long and crude.
And when you tire, feeling hopeless,
as the battle's far from through,
remember,
you are worth the world to me.
A stranger,
although himself still *lost and skewed,*
is hoping that you'll find your way.
And with love,
I'll find mine too.

...HOW beautiful the COLOR

The wonder and SURPRISE

A GIFT that could BE had

if BUT I'd OPEN UP

THIS my eyes.

shroud could soon be LIFTED

if I'd take the chance and try

If I'd FINALLY LET MY heart

that light believe

IS God and GUIDE

The Light

...How beautiful the color,
the wonder and surprise.
A gift that could be had
if I'd but open up my eyes.
This shroud could soon be lifted
if I'd take the chance and try.
If I'd, finally, let my heart believe
that light is God and guide.

If you are anywhere even close to where I was and need help, please go find it. Bottling up your emotions and trying to battle your demons on your own, for the sake of your pride, doesn't serve anyone. Rewriting your internal narrative, as mentioned before, is absolutely possible; *and is an essential part of growth and development.* However, in order to do that you need to acquire some new perspectives. But where do you get those if not from other people?

It doesn't have to be a therapist that you turn to, although that is a very good option. It could be anyone; family, friends, loved ones, and even complete strangers through something like podcasting or books. Whatever it may be, it doesn't matter, as long as you are getting what you need. Sometimes if you're lucky, though, the perfect person will drop into your life right when you need them the most. In many ways, that's what happened to me.

I had been slowly changing for a while, growing more and more tired of my own bullshit. However, I was still locked in some pretty negative thought patterns and bad habits. I had been researching a lot, looking for answers and better perspectives, but I was regularly butting heads with my deeply seeded beliefs about love, life, God, and everything else. I was staunchly atheist, incredibly nihilistic, and still believed that love wasn't actually real, or at least that I wasn't worth it. But that's when I met Ellen.

She was exactly who I needed at the time, and I think that I was the same for her. Although our relationship didn't last forever, I don't necessarily think that it was ever supposed to. It can be an uncomfortable idea to grasp sometimes, but not everything in life is meant to be permanent. That doesn't mean you shouldn't love and appreciate it while it's there though. Some things are just better left to divine timing. *Going with the flow will serve you well.* That is a fact I can no longer deny.

I want to be clear, though, that there was nothing magical or otherworldly about her. She was just a fun-loving, faithful girl who gave all of her heart to me freely, at a time that I desperately needed it. A time that I didn't think I even deserved it, and when love was the very thing that I was running from the most. If it wasn't for the unshakable feeling that I got when I was around her, *that I needed to know her,* I probably would have avoided our connection like I had with many others. But I shudder to think where I would be if that had been the case. *You should listen to those promptings when they come.*

She was so good to me, and I will always be grateful for her. But what I found the most influential was how she often acted as a mirror, reflecting by the way she lived her day-to-day, exactly what I had been missing. But even more so, she helped me see the parts of myself that I had forgotten almost entirely about, or had simply grown blind to.

I had spent so much time judging myself and building up a disdain for the unsavory aspects of life, that in many ways they were all that I could see. But where I saw the shade, she saw the light and she basked in it. Which by her nature, she applied to me. I was in the worst state physically, mentally, and emotionally that I had ever been, but yet she loved me wholly. She saw the good in me that I couldn't even recognize anymore, or just hadn't been giving myself any credit for. You would think that we would be the best judges of our own character, but we really aren't. Sometimes it's only through the eyes of others that we can honestly see ourselves, *and it's often better than we might assume.*

I had written a few poems before we met; digging up and getting out some of the shit I had buried, but was still bothering me. However, being a poet herself, she loved to hear them and was always encouraging me to write more. This, in turn, opened up the space in me to thoroughly explore what I had been so diligently trying to suppress. It was during that process that the bulk of my emotional healing took place. I would encourage you to write too, if you have never given it a go. It can be quite powerful.

However, as I began to release some of these things, *and soften my hardened heart,* it became clear to me that I had been judging myself and my frustrations with life a little too harshly. Furthermore, I had been placing blame for things unnecessarily, *beyond what was actually fair,* without ever stopping to celebrate the good or give it the attention that it deserved. Because, truthfully, it had been there all along, present in every situation. There was more than enough to go around, even in the worst of times. You just don't always see what you aren't looking for, unfortunately.

Gratitude is something that shouldn't be taken for granted. It's a practice, or perhaps a muscle of the mind, that if not utilized will be lost. I had heard of that concept before, but never really appreciated it, because remaining thankful when things are falling apart around you is very difficult. However, it's in those moments that maintaining a spirit of gratitude is most important. Because there are always two sides to every event, both good and bad, and when you focus on the good, the good is what you will find. You can and should acknowledge the bad when it's there, and learn whatever lessons it has to teach you. But it is gratitude that will quickly bring you back to peace.

Turning this corner in my understanding has been revolutionary for me, despite how simple it may seem. I thank Ellen so much for being such a wonderful example. It has allowed me to let go of my long-held resentments, forgiving everyone for everything that has ever stung. Moreover, it has enabled me to release the heavy judgments of myself that I have had for the times that I have hurt them. I had been holding on to all of that for way too long.

By far though, the most wonderful thing has been opening back up and drawing closer to myself, to my family and father, and to God, *whatever exactly that is.* I had pulled back quite a lot from all of them while in pursuit of my own *destruction.* However, those relationships, in all of their imperfection, are what I wouldn't trade for anything in the world. They are what is most valuable. I hope to never forget that fact again.

Throughout this section, *The Light,* I have included a mix of poems from that transitional period. Although it's difficult to convey every thought and changing emotion, I have tried my best. *I pray it does some good.*

Not Nothing

The majority of life is dull.
Existence is mostly empty space.
A *nothing*-ridden oddity,
though,
dark embrace.
That sets the perfect stage
to spark a life,
and breed a happiness
that lights up all its days,
and then, to call those days *good*.

Although they fade away
and fall to time,
too soon replaced,
know: that cascading light was you,
the beauty *-nothing-* created.

Idyll-d Eyes

There is never any shame in being wrong,
unless you can't admit to what is right.
When confronted with the truth,
if that can't sway you,
then nothing ever will.
And you'll be blinded
by the lies left yet to tell.
To sell a dream of
-an idol of a vision-
a wished, idyllic wisdom.
And it might feel as real as times before.
But you won't live near truth anymore.

But, damn, sometimes it's really hard to tell.

There is a Reason

I was falling apart almost entirely.
Withering away before my own very eyes.
But still, somehow, managed to stand tall, tiredly.
There were no more tears left to cry.
Although battered, bruised
from my own anxiety,
I still hoped to live, *or hoped to try.*
Because I realized I could further wilt,
and die here quietly.
Waste my heart and gifts with no goodbye,
and never know the reason for my life
and how it's guided me.
Or, I could right myself, *and find out why.*

Waste my **HEART**
and **GIFTS** with **NO GOODBYE,**
and never know
the **REASON** for my life
AND HOW IT'S guided me.
Or, I could right myself,
and find out why.

By Experience

When down in dire,
lowly straits,
I had to receive
to learn to give.
One day,
when I finally die,
I'll know what it means to live.

You Just Have to Look for Heaven

Silver winter water
with a bronze-lit, clouded sky.
I can't figure a better gift,
for *God-turned* eyes like mine.

The energy was right this morning.
The energy was "write" this morning.
I don't think I had a say,
but either way, I wouldn't change it.
This energy felt quite important,
as if a guiding thought
or hint,

 "It is time to get your life in order.
Here's a chance to take a grip.
You could continue sinking,
sailing,
trailing,
further lost, adrift.
Or maybe you could come *home,*
and cherish your life for what it is.
A God-damn masterpiece."

Frankly, I should be thanking
either Him, or what that is.
I got to see another day today.
How was I ever not grateful for this?

TO GET YOUR LIFE IN ORDER.

CHANCE TO TAKE A GRIP.

...OULD CONTINUE SINKING, SAILING,

...AILING, FURTHER LOST, ADRIFT.

OR MAYBE YOU COULD COME HOME,

AND CHERISH YOUR LIFE FOR WHAT IT IS

A GOD DAMN MASTERPIECE.

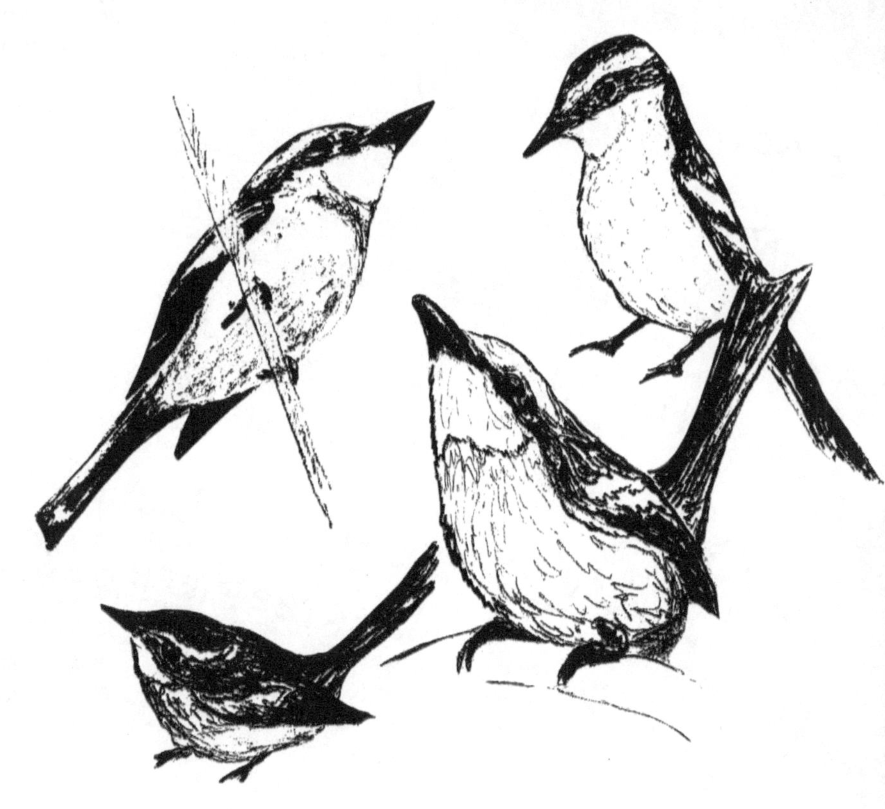

I wonder if that scares them.
I wonder if they stress sometimes,
like, "I don't know what's there.
I should turn back.
I think I've changed my mind."

Don't Get too Lost to Fly

Birds will spread their wings to fly,
and ride the wind to where it goes.
Whether tree or mountain high,
their future's never told.
They could go anywhere.

I wonder if that scares them.
I wonder if they stress sometimes,
like, "I don't know what's there.
I should turn back.
I think I've changed my mind."

But maybe they don't think.
Maybe they just trust their wings
and take a flight.
Maybe stress is just a people thing.
A curse of having bigger minds.

Birds developed wings.
They're free
to go get lost
and find their *hope*.
We get lost in imagination.
But like the birds,
we'll always need the Earth
to find *home*.

Home

One can build a room,
but it's the people there
who make the place.
Create a home or business
with their time to trade.
Create a space for living well
with spirit in the walls.
Where art is hung
and books are shelved,
there's dancing in the hall.
The world responds to us.

Fly Forever

I see these little creatures buzzing,
whirling,
tangled in their twisted time.
I know not what they're doing,
but to them, that's life.
I'm sure they're fine.
There is no rhyme or reason
to their silent dance
that comes to mind.
But the way they flutter
sings of joy.
No time is wasted.
Not even mine.

It's strange
how I could see,
but never notice them.

Gentle Giants

I never paid much mind
to the giants right outside my window.
That dance and wave with glee
in each and every way the wind blows.
It's strange how I could see,
but never notice them.
It's strange how I can breathe,
but never know the *friends*
who make this life here possible.
They're givers in the purest form.
Parents in a loving sense,
who build a home
and give forth fruit,
so that we may live a day again.
And again.
And again.
They don't stop giving.

A Reluctant Glow

The sunlight lingers over the horizon,
as if it fears to let the darkness take control.
But reluctantly it dissipates like fire wanes,
and then the starlight falls in place,
like it's found home.

Why must there always be opposition
to the opposite?

Shhh...

There is something so beautiful
about the daylight turning dark.
About the world falling asleep.
About the sky shimmering stars
all around us.
Perhaps it's just the change of scene.
An altered mood,
like winter's spring.
Just now,
we're being blessed
with the perspective of the shadows.
It's quiet here.

Positive Affirmations

You're it.
You're worth it.
You've been enough.
This *hatred* has been coming from yourself,
and yes,
it's made things tough.
Your anger's a reaction,
and lately you've been cuffed to it.

But...
You just need to relax, son.
You just need to keep things fun.
You're a light,
with shining bravado
and although you've rusted some,
you can polish up.
You can choose to love.
You can be anything that you want to,
and that time has come.
So do it now.

Prove to yourself that you're not a coward,
and that you deserve this.
That you are worth the world,
and that you are perfect
just the way you are.
And although that might seem far-fetched,

know, that you're not shooting for the stars.
The aim is just to be a better person.
And you're on that path.
So keep it true,
because you deserve this.

Damned

Damn, I've changed.
It hasn't been that long,
but, God damn, it's not the same.
I keep looking through old pictures.
Shocked,
in awe,
about how life's switched up.
Because this is nothing like I thought it'd be.

No, this isn't what I dreamed of.
This is what my late-night-working,
kind of, sort of sober self could scheme up.
Because the cards are different in reality,
and the games will change.
But I'll keep playing
until it costs me my beating heart.

I just hope I have a good run,
with some good funds,
and something to believe in.
But here now, lately, that's been ticking up.
Because now I'm with this really sweet girl,
but every day I'm scared I'll fuck it up.
I've fucked things up before
so,
my odds aren't good that I can keep this luck.

Can something be too pure?
Too good? Too good to know?
Because it's been good.
God damn it's good.
I'm not sure if I deserve it though.

Because I could be the one
that's she's been dreaming of.
The one to lift her up.
But I could also be the one to break her heart,
and now I'm nervous.
I told myself I wouldn't fall again,
but damn,
I think she's really worth it.
What we have is close to perfect.

But, truly, only time will ever tell.
And I'll be damned if things don't
go as they're supposed to.

Found It

I opened up to the world
and I found love.
I found connection.
I found purpose for the minutes
that keep ticking by.
I'm content in this.

I found love.
I found the light beyond the shadows.
I've seen the daylight come and go,
and I've found freedom in these golden hours.

I've found love.
I found a way to lift the weight
up off of my shoulders.
I've found help.
I've found safety from these storms,
by finding shelter
and protecting myself.
Because I've found love,
and I'd rather not just squander it.
Every day I learn its value
by comparing it to counterfeits.

I found love.
It's been pure and it's been good.
So I'll try my best to nourish it,

keep it alive, it's worth the world.
It's something I would die for,
and that's new for me,
but true.

But to be truthful,
if I died today,
I'd hope to never have a clue.
Because I don't think I'd rest in peace
while knowing well of hatred too.
Knowing that it's brewed in me.
Its remnants through and through,
throughout my life
I've watched it,
let it,
tear myself apart.
I've been so selfish.
Breaking down
and delving deep into the dark.

But I guess that's part of life.
And although I'm still not sure if I deserve it,
I've found love,
and it is everything worth living for.

Find It

If you open up to the world
you might find love.
Might find connection.
Might find purpose for the minutes
that keep ticking by,
until you're content in this.

You might find love,
and then the light beyond the shadows.
As the daylight comes and goes,
you can find your freedom in those golden hours.

You might find love,
or find the many ways to lift the weight
up off your shoulders
when you need help.
You'll find safety from these storms,
by finding shelter
and protecting yourself.
Because when you find love,
you really shouldn't squander it.
Every day you can learn its value
by comparing it to counterfeits.

When you find love,
it should be pure and should be good.
You should try your best to nourish it.

Keep it alive,
it's worth the world.
It is something that's worth dying for,
and if that's new for you,
it's true.

But being truthful...
If you died today,
would you hope to have a clue?
Do you wonder if you'd rest in peace
if you've known well of hatred too?
Knowing that it's brewed in you.
Its remnants through and through,
throughout your life,
as you have watched it,
let it,
tear yourself apart.
We've all been selfish.
Breaking down
and delving deep into the dark.

But I guess that's part of life;
even if you're not sure if you deserve it.
Go find love.
Because it is everything worth living for.

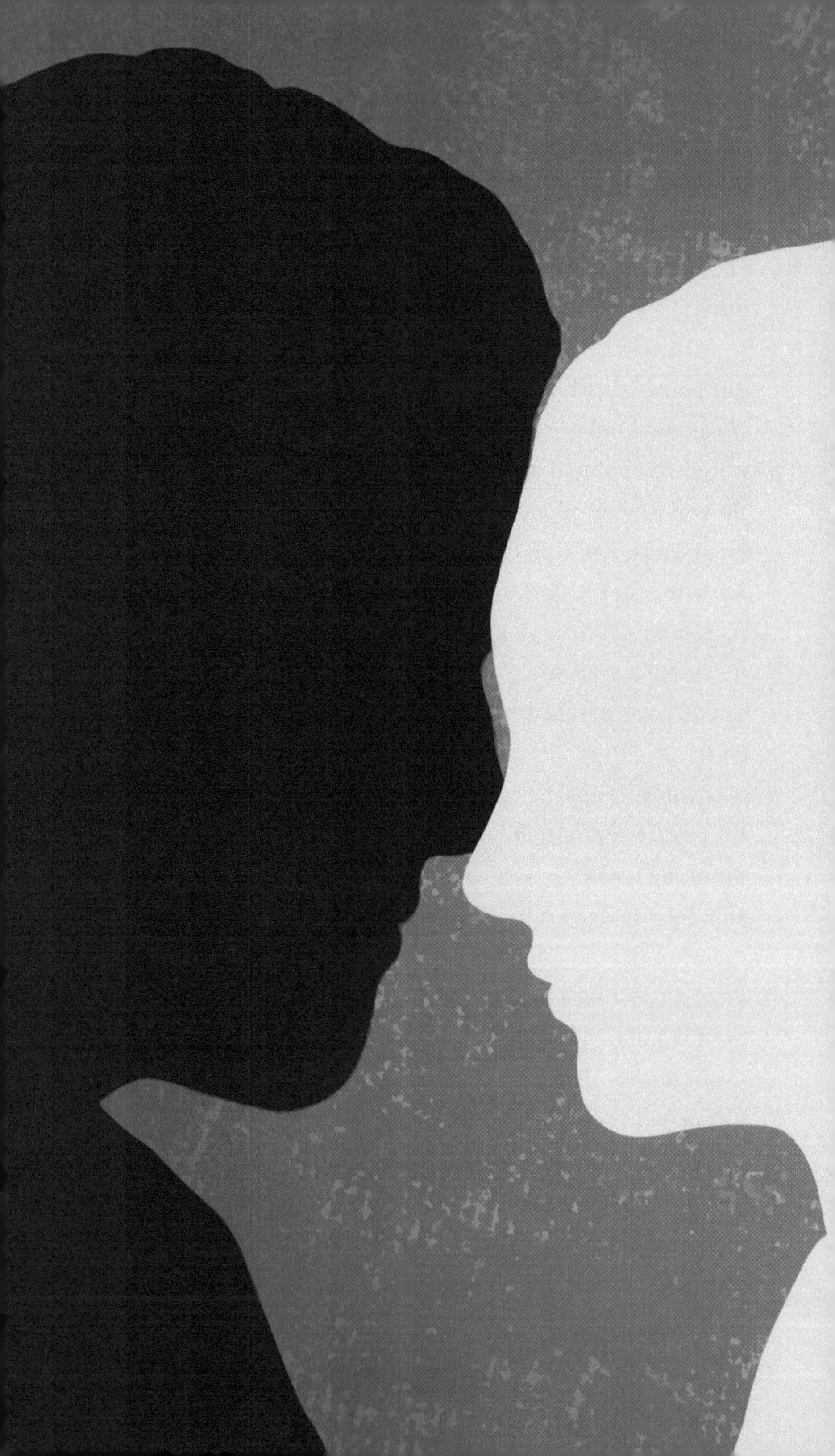

Flower Girl

I love how you don't mind
the taste of whiskey on my lips.
You'd rather just be connected to me.

I love how we've been sharing time.
It's obvious your love is free.
You've been really good for me.

I love how you're excited
for every waking hour.
It's good to see.
Because that *showering* of your *perfection*
has been helping plant the seeds
of a good natured,
new-found content.
A positivity
that I've been missing lately.

Lately,
I've been going crazy,
with my twisted thoughts
consuming me.
But with you I find a calmer storm.
With you I find a life that's warm.
I'm glad I introduced myself.

I'm glad you fell to my heart's spell,

the same I fell for you.
I hope these moments last forever.
I *hope* that we'll remain together.
I'll try to keep you as happy as can be.

But no matter what,
you already will be.
Because that's just who you are.
And I love you for that.

Grateful

"I am grateful for you!
I am grateful for you!!
I am grateful for you!!!
I would say it a million times
to get it stuck in your head."

And I broke down in tears.
I didn't think that it would hit me,
but yet it cut deep.
Grazing the heart left in me,
with such a soft and gentle edge.
I hope you know how much that meant.

I am the one who should be grateful.
But for you.

YOU showed me
just how good
a HEART could be.

Let Us Live Like You

You gave me so much love
when I was at my worst, ever.
You showed me just how good a heart could be.
I think you might have saved me
from myself...
Because I thought
that I was better off not caring...
About damn near anything.

I was weathered by depression.
Fatigued by heavy schedules.
But every day you shined,
reminding me to cherish life.
You're a leader by example.
I'll always love you for that.

CAPS LOCK

"I LOVE YOU IN ALL CAPS,"
you said to me
while pressed against my chest,
with your fingers *run* down my back.
You are the purest I've ever known,
and this moment,
is a gift that with time has grown.
And though these minutes will turn to hours,
I'd spend them all
if to just keep holding you.

But if I could
I would make time stop.
So that forever
with my caps locked,
you'd know the truth,
-with our hearts in tune-
that, "I LOVE YOU TOO."

• • •

There are movers
and there are shakers.
But you,
you are a lifesaver, my dear.

NEVER

If you've had my heart,
you'll have it forever.
Or at least a part of it.
You're something that I never will forget.

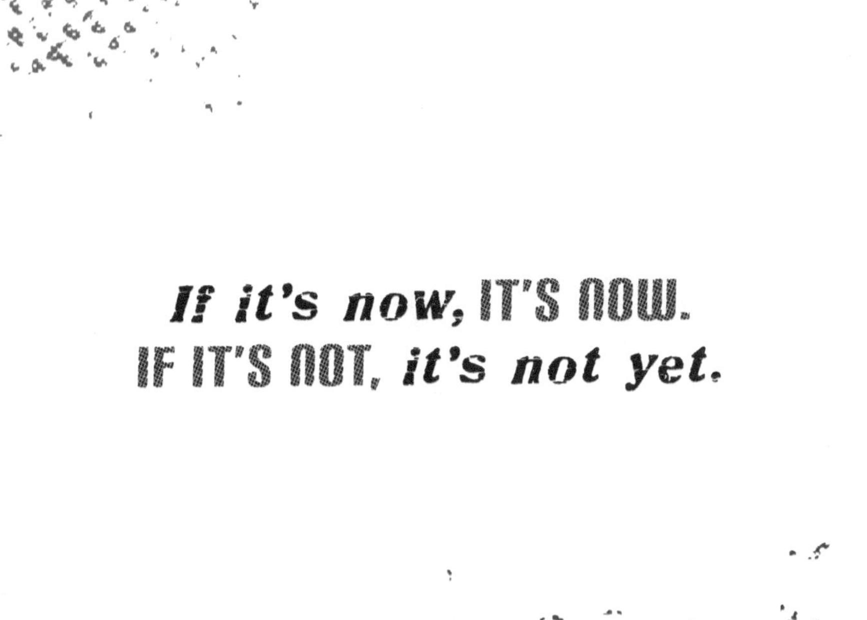
If it's now, IT'S NOW.
IF IT'S NOT, it's not yet.

Again

Bare walls and brown boxes,
I guess it's time to move again.
This makes the eleventh time
that I've restarted and lost some friends.
You'd think by now that I'd be good at it.
You'd think by now it wouldn't hurt.
But I guess I'm not an expert
in the art of hearts,
and of not giving a fuck.

Sometimes I think I feel too much.

You'd think that I'd stop caring.
You'd think by now I might have learned,
but every time I've tried,
deep inside it just felt worse.
So I guess I just have to sit with it,
and keep my focus on the future.
So I can make the life I'd like to live,
and soon,
just start living.
But first, again,
I've got to move these damn boxes.

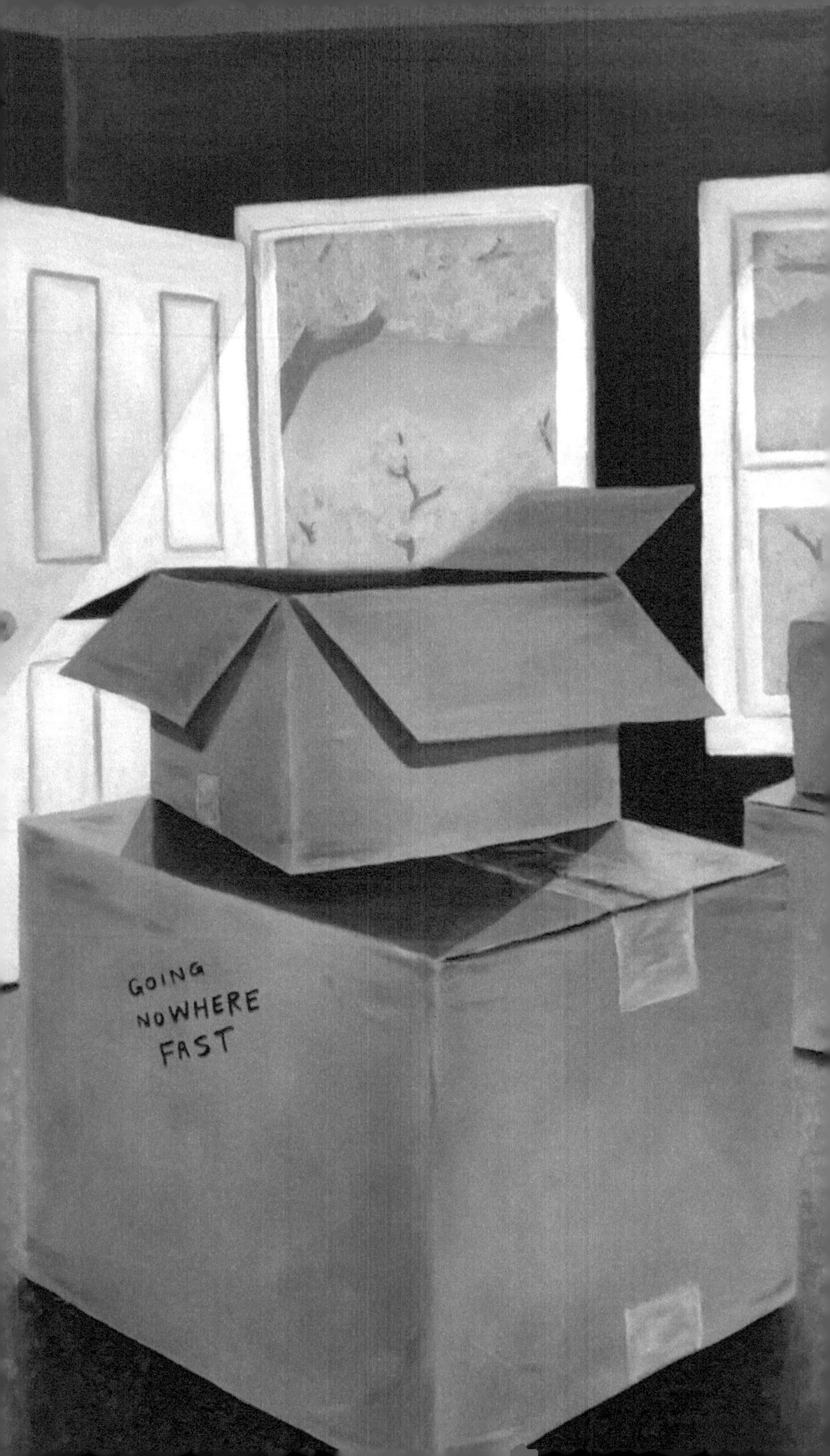

GOING
NOWHERE
FAST

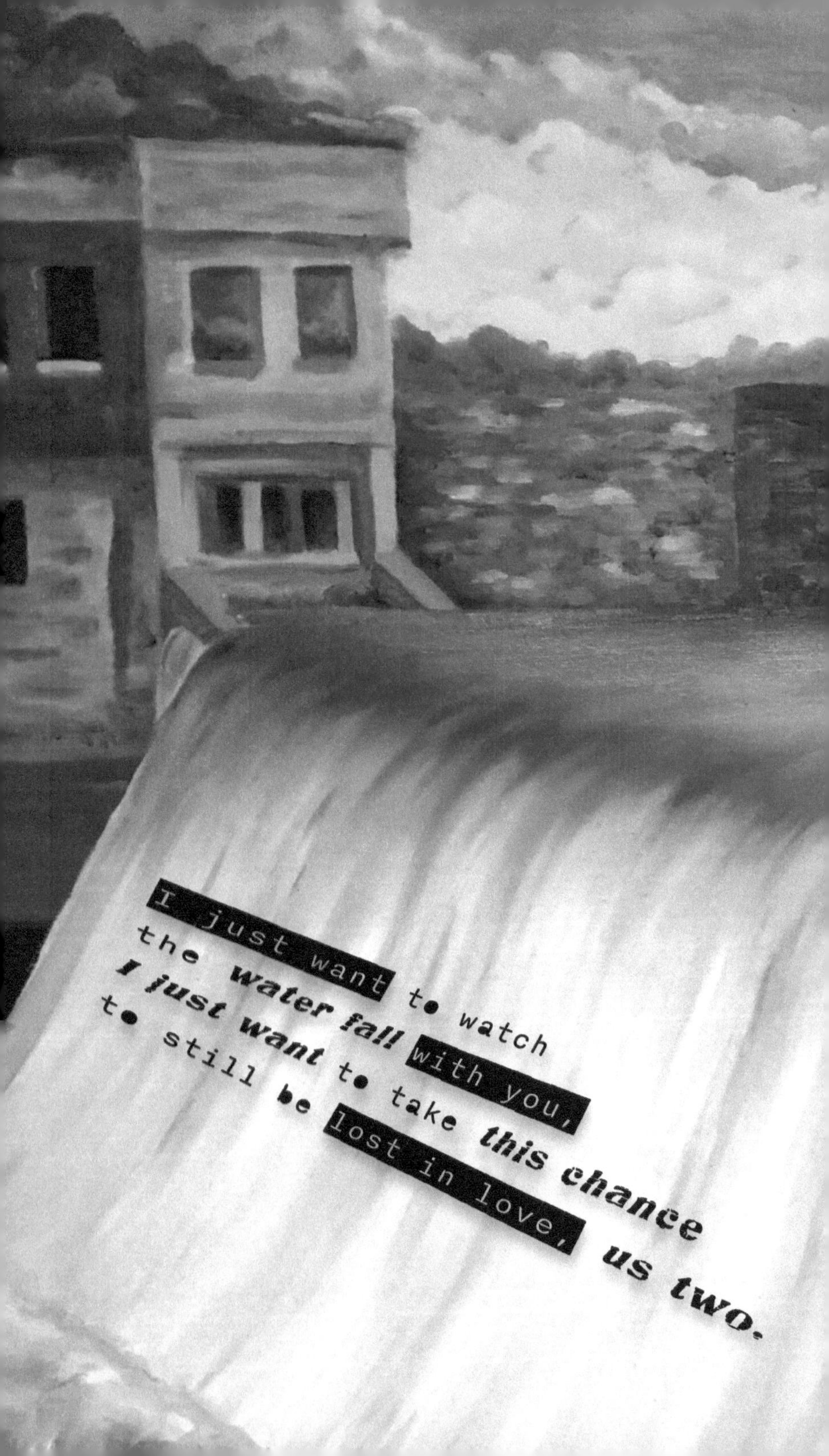

I just want to watch
the water fall with you,
I just want to take this chance
to still be lost in love, us two.

Let's Go Back to Walter Hill

I can't forget my camera.
We need to take a few more pictures.
That way I won't forget your smile,
or the way the sunlight hits you
as it reflects back, by the dam.
One last time,
let's go back.
Take each other by the hand,
and maybe dance to the songs the birds sing.
Or, just sit and talk about our plans;
our lives ahead of us.

I just want to watch the water fall with you.
I just want to take this chance
to still be lost in love, us two.

I'm going to miss you,
and I know you feel same.
So let's go back to Walter Hill,
one final time,
and shoot a frame-
-a moment you and I can smile back on,
every time our hearts start saying,
"Let's go back to Walter Hill."

I wish our dance in the gazebo,
under the starlight,
never ended.
It might have been my favorite time with you,
and I don't like to dance.

It might have been
the pond, the trees, the birds and things,
surrounding just us two.
But as I think,
all I see is you.

All I feel is your hand in mine,
our bodies pressed, near glued.
And how I had hoped
that maybe, it'd last a lifetime.

And although it hurts, knowing the truth,
that our time is up.
I'll always have that dance.
"And it's all because of you."

Lovely Lady

Getting over her felt near impossible,
until I met you.
Getting over you might feel the same.
But somehow this time,
I know I'll be okay.

But that doesn't mean that I won't miss you.
I surely do.
You've imprinted with your heart and hands,
and I still feel you.

Although with each new day, a little less.
I'd be hard pressed
to ever forget the love you gave me.
I'll always love you, lovely lady.

Hold My Hand

Waking next to you,
I had always been the early riser.
Maybe 'cause my dreams don't sleep,
or maybe I was dying to see you.
I can't be sure.
But I'd never try to wake you,
because I'd hate to see
that gift of life
begin evading you, too.
I hope you'll always sleep well.
So, I'd let you take your time.
But I'd wonder where you were,
what you were seeing
through those starry eyes,
-while I was there entangled
by a stream of thoughts
or star of mine-
sitting on that bed,
some days closer to the edge
than even I realized...
You'd wake up,
hold out your hand for mine,
and bring my world back into focus
with a sunny gaze:
your loving smile.

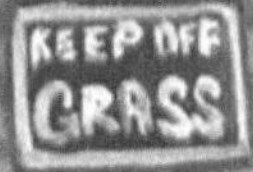

I'd wonder where you were,
what you were seeing
through those starry eyes,
-while I was there entangled
by a stream of thoughts
or star of mine-

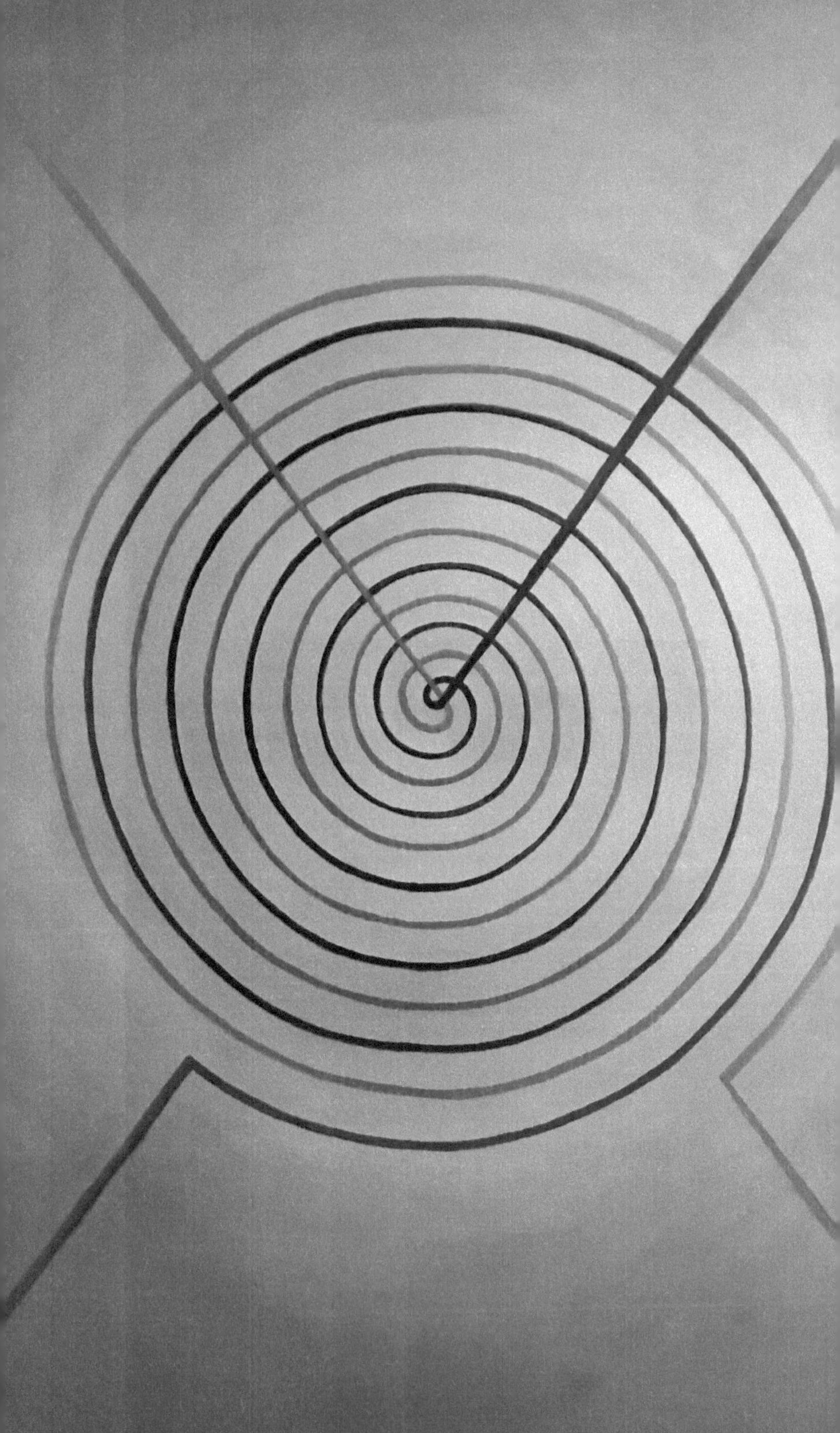

Crossing Paths

Loving you was easy.
I never felt I had to play pretend.
We had so much in common,
you, *so quickly*, became my best friend.
Near two years had passed,
as if *it* free in the wind.
Time had flown so fast
I barely noticed it.
-It was well spent-
But, our lives followed their paths.
Our true directions never bowed.
The dance we danced soon halted,
as we traveled our different roads.
It's a shame things had to change,
still now, I can't pretend.
But if there's one thing that I've learned,
it's that
all good things come to an end.
I am just,
forever grateful
for the time we got to spend.
I am wishing you well, always.
My lover, my best friend.

GENTLE TERMS

I watched the weather *wind in*
white walled whispers,
that glowed a subtle grin before the rain.
That danced a certain dance
that bounced their light back through the shade.
And spoke in gentle terms,
reminding me I'll be okay.
"It's just the rain."
"It's just the price for life we pay."

Step by Step

I'm near convinced
that all things happen for a reason.
I feel impressed by certain timing and tact.
Almost, as if,
life is but a journey
through an unknown plain.
With little hints of guidance,
as a somewhat trodden path,
directing me to God knows where.
And although I'm often looking back,
it's best to just keep walking.

I have been *blessed* with *hardship.*
Gifted with *frustration.*
Loved enough *to* *learn* *to* *grow,*
and *taught* to *garner hope*
in my *darkest* *moments.*

Only if You Allow it

Pondering life
and all of its hardships,
I used to think in terms of,
"Why is this happening to me?"
"What have I done to deserve this?"
"If God is love, then why do I feel this way?"

But, frankly, I was quite naive.
In my life,
I have been blessed with hardship.
Gifted with frustration.
Loved enough to learn to grow,
and taught to garner hope
in my darkest moments.
Because the light will always shine through,
if you allow it to.

Never Hesitate to Speak

I silenced myself
for the hearts of others.
I learned to fake a smile,
so no one felt my pain.
I ran from all things "good" I'd learned,
so that "good" can't hurt again.

But in that process,
I did lose myself.
In that process
I lost friends.
The fruits that bore from seeds I'd sewn
cursed, "NEVER LOVE AGAIN."

My veins then bled
with whiskey pure,
and my lungs
found smoke, no end.
I nearly died at least three times,
but could not care.
Because "I" already felt dead.

It wasn't until a gentle soul,
who loved *me for me,*
once said,
"You're a light, so be a light.
Because, you can't see

the good that you've always been.
I love your mind and I love your heart,
but your soul needs time, *so spend it.*"

Not as if to judge,
she never could.
She is the good that I once fled.
But she *saved my life,*
reminding me,
not of who I was, but who I am.

A light.
A mind.
A heart.
A soul.
A life with time to spend.

And I can see it now,
so clearly now.
And for that,
I WILL ALWAYS LOVE YOU ELLEN.

Either way,
I was lost and dazed,
SCRAPING for *grains of truth.*
I had to slow down.

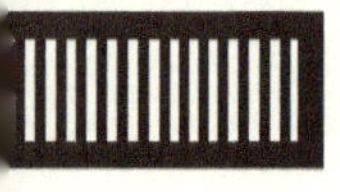

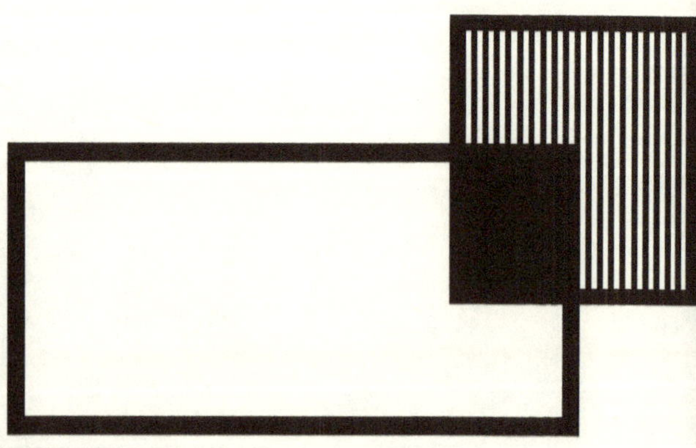

RE-CONNECTION

I spent the better part of a decade,
looking for any way to spite *a* god.
Looking for any reason to abandon
the "good things" taught to me.
I didn't believe them.
I never believed them.
How could any of this be the case?
How come God might talk to you,
but never treated me the same?
I couldn't hear it.
And what had I done to deserve this?
-Absent of God and father-
I was a good kid,
but I felt abandoned often.
And in my head, without their blessings,
how could anyone ever love me?
Somehow, I couldn't even love myself.
At times I think I found Hell.
But,
despite the depths of my despair
I traveled on,
trudging paths in *wrong directions,*
trying to find a life of dreams,
despite what was intended.
But pleasure's pretty cheap
and builds a worldly, weak perspective.
So that shattered too.

Or maybe I just outgrew it.
Either way,
I was lost and dazed,
scraping for grains of truth.
I had to slow down.
I had to take a few steps back,
because it wasn't *truth* that led me here.
I avoided most trodden paths,
and refused to even aim in their same direction.
I guess I thought I knew better.
But,
through thought-spelled whispers
and subtle urges,
I have been being guided back.
And with enough time
and opportunity,
to quiet down and listen,
it has become irrefutable to me
that something is there.
Something hears me.
That,
somehow,
"life" is "it."
"Love" is too,
and it is beautiful.
It is tragic.
It is all things worthy of a tale,
and perhaps,
that's why I can't stop listening.

True Godly Type

I think most works of art stem from
a dying wish to be remembered.
As if it's a mark left on the world,
to be cherished by those who come after us.
And you know what,
those artists *should* be cherished.
At least those deserving of it,
based on skill, or diversity of thought,
whatever is deemed acceptable...
And if that's ever my work, great.
I hope it does something for you.
It would mean the world to me if it does.
But, honestly, the people I look up to
are the quiet type,
calm and mild,
who live their life without ever
giving an honest fuck at all.
Those who know their beauty,
and who are brave enough to let it die with them.
They are the true godly types.

Art

Everyone should cherish art,
hang it on their walls,
and share it far.
Because art is MORE than just what's seen.
It's the subtle dance of friendship.
It's the flutter when two lovers kiss.
It's the grace and good of all that is.
It's both everything,
and nothing,
and that is exactly why it's gorgeous.

They'll Come and Go

If someone never comes back into your life,
they've served their purpose.
But if they come back,
you've made a friend.
Try your best to make them grin.
We're all not so different.

Believe

No true creator would make something, just to cast it away. No, *not the creator of love*. However, since we do have freewill, we have every capacity to despise ourselves and live in disgrace. But we also have the opposite. *Be Love*.

It's in everybody. It's in everything. We all have the proclivity for right and wrong, and the ability to let either fester. Our thoughts are not who we are, but we can become what we obsess over. It could be hatred, it could be grief, it could be anger, or any mimic of release. *Or it could be love*. It could be generosity, curiosity. You could be the light that shines above. You make the choice.

Love may be the easiest thing in the world to do, but it's also the hardest thing to accept, or admit that you deserve. *But you are it*. You just need to let it free and let it flourish.

BE LOVE.

And even though
I know *with time*
my life will *start to fade,*
my God, these moments
make it *worth it.*

Once a Distant Prayer

Life isn't so bad
when you find some distance from it.
When you learn how to keep on standing
through your conflicts;
when you can look up to the sky
and feel your troubles drift away.
It's in *those* moments
that I learned how to truly pray.
It's in those moments
that I truly learned to know myself.
And even though I know
with time
my life will start to fade,
my God,
these moments
make it worth it.

Aged Like Wine

When I was young
I thought I learned it all,
that I had seen life deal its hand.
Because it's true that as a child
nothing *ever* went to plan.

I had watched things fall apart,
time and time and time again.
But with time came bigger questions,
for things I couldn't understand.

I started to get angry.
That feeling started to expand.
But what made things so much worse,
I missed the hell out of you Dad.

I thought at times you didn't love us.
I thought at times that love was damned.
But I never really knew you,
until I grew to be a man.

I don't hold a thing against you.
I no longer can be mad.
Because I've seen the truth
of how life tempts us,
and how strong you must have been
for the longest time.

I'm sure you have regrets
that to this day still make you sad.
But know, I really do still love you,
and I am proud to call you Dad.

I should tell you this more often.
I should tell you all the time.
And I'm sorry this was bottled up,
but this truth
has aged liked wine.

Love is Life

Do you want to know God?
Look up to the sky.
Do you want to know God?
Dream upon a starry night.

Because if you're desperate in your search,
beyond this Earth, I'm sure you'll find *it*.
But if you really want to know God,
first know yourself, *it* is what's life.

(You'll learn to love it.)

If you're *desperate*
in your search,
beyond this Earth,
I'm sure you'll find it.

KEEP HOPE

These days it seems like,
despite our bells and whistles,
we never let our freedom ring.
Despite our mics that amplify,
we never hear a heart that sings.
Despite abundant wisdom,
no one ever seems to know a thing.
These days seem empty.

I've noticed things seems scarce among the plenty.
Like our flame has turned to ash.
And while our gold has turned to cash,
we just keep spending.
All in hopes we'll get it back.
But this cycle is never ending.

We've amended what it means to live.
We've stolen what was meant to give.
We've dabbled in the finer things,
forgetting their expense,
and our pocket's empty,
so our freedom has turned to debt.

These days seem like they're failing.
Like we're fading out,
curtailing growth,
but somehow I'm still keeping hope.

Hope for the future.
Hope that love can overcome
the bitter cold in all of us.
Hope for the good *that's bound to come.*
Keep hope.
Move forward,
with a focus on our dreams,
never letting the world keep us down.

Keep hope.
Keep going.
Keep heart in mind
and mind in soul,
and soon the negative will rope in.

Keep hope.

We'll Be Okay

I am nothing but a young man
with a lot of opinions,
and perhaps a wisdom beyond my years.
A wisdom enough to know
that I know nothing,
which has been a major fear of mine.
But lately me and "God,"
we've been okay.
I don't have to know "all truth" today.
Perhaps, I'll look up at the sky
and just enjoy it.

A letter
to my readers.

There is a funny feeling that I have swelling within me while writing this letter; wrapping up years of my life and sending it out into the world. It's somewhere between stress and excitement. Because I have gone over these ideas a million times or more, trying to find the right words to say. Fearful of giving away too much, while worrying that I haven't said enough, all the same; *as if I could ever describe it fully.* But I'm also delighted, because what I have said might just go on to serve a purpose. It definitely did for me.

There is nothing that I could ever write that would change a life though. Only you can change you. I wouldn't want to have that kind of power over anyone anyway. The beauty of this existence is derived from individuality. *The contrast.* That's why it's so important that we all live as our truest selves. We compliment each other when we do.

When we are out of alignment with who we really are, we find ourselves in trouble *in every aspect of our lives.* It could be career, love, friends, hobbies, habits, location, or lifestyle. All of it is important, and usually if one is out of balance then the others follow suit. You shouldn't be afraid of authenticity, or of pursuing the things you love to do. You wouldn't be who you are if you weren't supposed to be. However, how you are acting may be far from who that actually is. Sometimes we have to do a thorough and honest audit of ourselves to find out where we stand.

That is why I would encourage you to write. When things are running amuck, jot them down. It can be in poetry, journaling, or even scratch notes on a napkin. It doesn't matter, as long as it helps to organize the thoughts that are swirling. Tell your story to yourself as if you're someone who gives a damn, and you'll be amazed by the clarity of your new perspectives. *I promise you that.* You don't have to write a book though. You don't have to be a writer at all. You just have to be willing to be truthful with yourself.

I hope one day to live in a world that isn't so disjointed. A world where everyone has a dream that they live all of the way through, *instead of just existing in all of the ways that aren't their truth.* Which, in the end, is an extension of God, or the Universe, or whatever you'd like to call it. *That infinite thing that thrives with diversity.* Creating you and billions of others with their own, unique hopes, loves, passions, and joys. All of which can shine a light brighter than we ourselves could ever see. You owe it to the world to allow that light to shine, but you owe it to yourself just the same. I wish you all of the happiness there could ever be.

Life can be tragic.
But the greatest dramas
make for the greatest stories.
And if that is what my life can be,
a great story,
then truly, I have
nothing to be fearful of at all.

With Love,
Kevin

The End

The Beginning